The Mark Zuckerberg Story

Tom Christian

Level 5

IBC パブリッシング

はじめに

　ラダーシリーズは、「はしご（ladder）」を使って一歩一歩上を目指すように、学習者の実力に合わせ、無理なくステップアップできるよう開発された英文リーダーのシリーズです。
　リーディング力をつけるためには、繰り返したくさん読むこと、いわゆる「多読」がもっとも効果的な学習法であると言われています。多読では、「1.速く 2.訳さず英語のまま 3.なるべく辞書を使わず」に読むことが大切です。スピードを計るなど、速く読むよう心がけましょう（たとえばTOEIC®テストの音声スピードはおよそ1分間に150語です）。そして1語ずつ訳すのではなく、英語を英語のまま理解するくせをつけるようにします。こうして読み続けるうちに語感がついてきて、だんだんと英語が理解できるようになるのです。まずは、ラダーシリーズの中からあなたのレベルに合った本を選び、少しずつ英文に慣れ親しんでください。たくさんの本を手にとるうちに、英文書がすらすら読めるようになってくるはずです。

《本シリーズの特徴》
- 中学校レベルから中級者レベルまで5段階に分かれています。自分に合ったレベルからスタートしてください。
- クラシックから現代文学、ノンフィクション、ビジネスと幅広いジャンルを扱っています。あなたの興味に合わせてタイトルを選べます。
- 巻末のワードリストで、いつでもどこでも単語の意味を確認できます。レベル1、2では、文中の全ての単語が、レベル3以上は中学校レベル外の単語が掲載されています。
- カバーにヘッドホーンマークのついているタイトルは、オーディオ・サポートがあります。ウェブから購入/ダウンロードし、リスニング教材としても併用できます。

《使用語彙について》

レベル1:中学校で学習する単語約1000語

レベル2:レベル1の単語+使用頻度の高い単語約300語

レベル3:レベル1の単語+使用頻度の高い単語約600語

レベル4:レベル1の単語+使用頻度の高い単語約1000語

レベル5:語彙制限なし

Contents

Foreword 3

Part 1 A gifted youth 5

Part 2 The birth of Facebook 21

Part 3 Becoming a real company 43

Part 4 A giant of the Internet 69

Word List 94

読み始める前に

【読み進める上で知っておくと役に立つ単語】

- administrator
- automate
- crowd sourcing
- entrepreneur
- epic poem
- hacking
- implementation
- intoxicated
- lockdown
- mash
- mentor
- meritocratic
- registration
- robotic
- semester
- shabby
- tagline
- tipping point
- uprising
- villain

【登場人物】

Edward Zuckerberg エドワード・ザッカーバーグ 父。ユダヤ教徒。裕福な歯科医で、ニューヨーク郊外の自宅で開業している。

Karen Zuckerberg カレン・ザッカーバーグ 母。精神科医。出産を機に夫の歯科医院のマネージャーとなる。

Randi Zuckerberg ランディ・ザッカーバーグ 姉。後にFacebookのマーケティングディレクターを務める。この他にダナとアリエルの二人の妹がいる。

Cameron and Tyler Winkelvoss, and Divya Narendra ウィンクルヴォス兄弟とディヴィヤ・ナレンドラ ハーバード大学の先輩。最初にソーシャルサイトを立ち上げようとザックに持ちかける。ザックがそれとは別にFacebookを立ち上げたため、アイデアを盗まれたと主張。

Adam D'Angelo アダム・ダンジェロ 高校の同級生。ザックと共に音楽再生ソフトSynapseを開発する。FacebookではCTO（最高技術責任者）を務めた。

Eduardo Saverin エドゥアルド・サベリン 高校からの友人で、ハーバードでの同級生。ブラジル人でザックと同じユダヤ教徒。在学中に共同設立者となり、FacebookのCFO（最高財務責任者）とビジネスマネージャーを務めた。

Dustin Moskovitz ダスティン・モスコヴィッツ ハーバード大学時代のルームメイト。プログラミングは初心者であったが、膨大な作業時間でFacebookの設立と発展を助けた。後にFacebookのCTOを務めた。

Chris Hughes クリス・ヒューズ ハーバード大学時代のルームメイト。歴史や文学を好む。容姿端麗で、Facebookのスポークスマン的存在。

Sean Parker ショーン・パーカー コンピュータ界では伝説的プログラマー。ハッキングによる逮捕歴を持つ。ザックと意気投合し、彼のチームに加わる。

Peter Thiel ピーター・シール PayPalの設立者でありCEO（最高経営責任者）。Facebookに投資し、ディレクターとなる。

Sheryl Sandberg シェリル・サンドバーグ ハーバード大学卒業。世界銀行や財務省などで活躍した華々しい経歴を持つ女性。2008年にGoogleからFacebookへ移り、COO（最高執行責任者）を務める。

【マーク・ザッカーバーグとFacebookの変遷】

1984年	5月14日、ニューヨーク郊外の裕福な歯科医の家に生まれる。
1995年	ザック11歳のとき、コンピュータ・プログラムの家庭教師につく。
1996年	父のオフィスのためにZuckNetという簡易メッセージソフトを開発。
2000年頃	地元の高校から世界的に優秀と認められた有名校へ転入。Synapseという音楽再生ソフトを開発。
2002年	ハーバード大学へ入学。コンピュータ科学と心理学を専攻。
2003年	9月、Course Matchに続き、Facemashという学内生徒の容姿格付けサイトを公開し、物議を醸す。この頃、ウィンクルヴォス兄弟やナレンドラと出会う。
2004年	2月4日、Thefacebook.comを公開。ハーバード大学に加え、コロンビア大学、スタンフォード大学、イェール大学なども参加。
	4月、Thefacebookを法人とし、広告販売を始める。

2004年	夏、作業場所をカリフォルニアのパロアルトに移す。現在のFacebook本部。
2004年	9月、ピーター・シールから最初の投資となる50万ドルを受ける。
	秋、モスコヴィッツと共にハーバード大学を休学、後に退学する。
	11月、Thefacebookの登録者が100万人を突破。
2005年	ThefacebookからFacebookに改名。ショーン・パーカーが退社。
	秋、Facebookを高校生に公開。
2006年	新サービス"Work Networks"を発表。
	年末、Facebookが一般に公開される。新サービス"News Feed"を発表。
2007年	Facebook上で動作するアプリケーションを開発するためのプログラミングインターフェースであるFacebookAPIを公開。クリス・ヒューズが退社。
2008年	シェリル・サンドバーグが入社。日本語版Facebookが発表される。新サービス"Facebook Connect"が発表される。
	中頃、ウィンクルヴォス兄弟とナレンドラからの訴訟を受け、Facebook側が65百万ドルを支払う。
2009年	中国がFacebookにアクセス制限をかける。
2010年	ザックが男性ファッション誌の最もダサいセレブランキングで3位に選ばれる。
	10月、Facebook誕生秘話を描く映画 *The Social Network* が公開される。
	ザックがタイム誌のパーソンオブザイヤーに選ばれる。
2011年	新サービス"Timeline"を発表。12月、Facebookは70以上の言語に対応可能となる。
2012年	2月、Facebook登録者が8億4500万人を突破。

Cover photo: Facebook CEO Mark Zuckerberg delivers a keynote address at a conference in San Francisco, Wednesday, April 21, 2010. (AP Photo/Marcio Jose Sanchez)　AP/アフロ

The Mark Zuckerberg Story

Tom Christian

Foreword

From Harvard to the world

In 2004, nineteen-year-old Mark Zuckerberg started work on an online social network in his dormitory room at Harvard University.

It was called Thefacebook.

By 2012, just eight years later, over 900 million people belonged to Facebook. More than 12% of all the people in the world were members. The business was worth between $80 billion and $100 billion dollars. At twenty-eight, Mark Zuckerberg was already one of the richest people on the planet.

This is the story of how Mark Zuckerberg built Facebook—and changed the world.

Part 1

※

A gifted youth

A privileged childhood

Mark Elliot Zuckerberg was born on May 14, 1984, in Dobbs Ferry, a New York suburb. His father, Edward, was a rich and successful dentist who worked in the basement of the family's large house. His mother, Karen, was a psychiatrist. After she had children, she started working as her husband's office manager.

Mark was the second of four children. He had an older sister, Randi, (who later became marketing director of Facebook), and two younger sisters, Donna and Arielle.

It was Edward who first introduced Mark to computer programming. He even hired a private computer tutor for Mark when he was eleven. The tutor was a professional software developer named David Newman. Newman came to the Zuckerbergs' house once a week to give Mark lessons. He could not believe how fast Mark learned.

While he was still at high school, Mark went to a nearby university to take a programming course. The class was for graduate students. Edward took Mark into the classroom on the first day of the course. "You can't bring your son into the classroom with you," the teacher complained. "I'm not," replied Edward. "It's my son who's taking the class!"

Lots of children play computer games. Mark, however, was different. He actually made his own games. He had some friends who were good at drawing. When they came to his house to play, he used their pictures to create his own computer games.

Some of the programs the young Mark made were very useful. His dentist father didn't like the way his receptionist shouted, "There's a patient here, Dr. Zuckerberg," whenever a new patient came in. Mark, who was twelve at the time, decided to solve the problem. He designed an instant messaging system to connect all the computers in the house and office.

Thanks to Mark's system, the receptionist did not need to shout anymore. Instead, she sent a message telling Edward that a new patient had arrived. Mark called the system "ZuckNet." He made it in 1996, one year before AOL's Instant Messenger came out.

A very special high school

Mark transferred from Ardsley High School, a local public school, to Phillips Exeter for the last two years of high school. Phillips Exeter is an expensive private school founded in 1781. Notable former students include Dan Brown, the author of *The Da Vinci Code*; Peter Benchley, the author of *Jaws*; and Franklin Pierce, the 14th President of the

Part 1 A gifted youth

United States.

Phillips Exeter is also famous for using the "Harkness table" method of teaching. The classes are very small, and the students and teacher all sit together around a small oval table. The class is more like a discussion seminar than a lecture. The students get the chance to talk and debate.

At Phillips Exeter, Mark was the captain of the fencing team. His favorite subjects were Greek and Latin. He particularly liked the epic poems of Homer and Virgil.

Mark still loved programming. He and his classmate Adam D'Angelo created a program called Synapse for their final year project at Phillips Exeter. Synapse recognized the sort of music people listened to and suggested other songs they might like.

Microsoft and AOL were impressed with Synapse. Both companies offered to buy the software and give Mark a job. But he wasn't interested. In September 2002, he went to Harvard, the most prestigious university in the United States, to major in computer science and psychology.

Worst dressed man on campus

Zuckerberg was five feet eight inches (about 173 centimeters) tall, with curly reddish-brown hair and a pale face with freckles. Whatever the weather, he always wore the same shabby clothes: a T-shirt, a fleece jacket, baggy jeans or shorts, and rubber Adidas sandals.

(Zuckerberg didn't change his style of dressing even after Facebook became successful. That's why *Esquire*, a men's magazine, ranked him No. 3 in their "worst dressed celebrity" list in 2010.)

Zuckerberg was shy and quiet. He always took a long time to reply to questions. His answers were often short and ironic, and his voice was flat and expressionless. Some people said his short, robotic way of speaking was like an instant messaging system.

Everybody called him "Zuck."

Building websites for students

It was in Zuckerberg's second, or sophomore, year at Harvard that he started creating websites for the other students to use.

In the first week of the fall semester in September 2003, Zuckerberg made a website called Course Match. Zuckerberg realized that many students choose their courses not because they are interested in a subject, but because they want the chance to meet a cute boy or girl taking that course. With Course Match, people could click on a course to see

Zuckerberg in a Harvard sweatshirt
(Elaine Chan/Priscilla Chan)

who was taking it, or click on a person's name to see what courses he or she was taking. Course Match was very popular because it came out at the start of a semester. That's exactly when students choose their courses.

The drunken master

One month later, in October 2003, Zuckerberg started working on his next website idea. This one was called Facemash. ("Mash" is slang for to "mix up.") With Facemash, you could compare photographs of two Harvard students and vote which was the more attractive. (At first, Zuckerberg also planned to include some pictures of cows and pigs, but one of his roommates told him it was a bad idea.)

Zuckerberg started Facemash one night when he was upset after having an argument with a girl. We know that because he was blogging at the same time as he was programming the site. "— is a bitch," he wrote on his blog. "I need to think of something to take my mind off her. I'm a little intoxicated, I'm not going to lie."

Zuckerberg was drinking beer as he programmed Facemash. He completed the site in just eight hours, starting at 8 PM and finishing at 4 AM. Photographs of Harvard students were a key part of the site. Zuckerberg got the pictures by hacking into the servers of nine of Harvard's 12 student houses.

Zuckerberg launched Facemash in the afternoon of Sunday, November 2, 2003. He e-mailed the URL to his friends, asking them to have a look. Then he went out.

Getting into trouble

Zuckerberg returned to his room late that night. His computer had crashed because so many people had visited the Facemash site.

The problems were not just technical. Groups representing black and Hispanic women at Harvard complained that the site was "sexist" and "racist."

At 10:30 PM, the Harvard computer services department shut off Zuckerberg's access to the Internet. But 450 students had already visited Facemash and voted on 22,000 sets of photographs. People loved the site!

The administrators were not so pleased with Zuckerberg. He had broken the university's rules on privacy, security and copyright. He had to go and see a student counselor and say sorry to the women's groups. "The site was just an experiment," he said. "I never expected it to spread so fast."

Zuckerberg had been lucky. His punishment was lighter than he expected. When he got back to his room, he and his roommates celebrated by drinking a bottle of champagne.

A man of many projects

Zuckerberg was always working on some kind of software project. He kept a whiteboard in the passage outside his room in Kirkland House at Harvard. He used it to sketch out his ideas. "I had this hobby of building these little projects," he said later. "I had 12 projects in my second year. Mostly they were about seeing how people connected."

One of his projects was to build a website for the Association of Harvard Black Women (who had been upset by Facemash). Another was a special site that found how people mentioned in articles in the university newspaper were connected to his favorite computer science professor, Harry Lewis.

Zuckerberg never worried about breaking the rules. In the fall semester, for example, he had an exam about Roman art. The problem was he had hardly been to class. He therefore created a special website with pictures of the art from the course and e-mailed it to his classmates. "Hey, why don't you use this site to get ready for the exam by discussing the art," he wrote in the mail. Zuckerberg then read all the comments his classmates posted—and passed his exam easily.

Double trouble

In early November, an article about Mark Zuckerberg and Facemash appeared in the student newspaper, *The Harvard Crimson*. The article caught the attention of three final year students: Cameron Winkelvoss, Tyler Winkelvoss, and Divya Narendra.

Cameron and Tyler Winkelvoss were identical twins. Their family was rich, and they were tall, handsome and athletic. Their favorite sport was rowing. (In fact, they were so good at rowing that they represented America in the 2008 Beijing Olympics.) While the Winkelvoss twins were typical WASPs (White Anglo-Saxon Protestants), their friend Divya Narendra was the son of Indian immigrants.

For about 10 months, Narendra and the Winkelvoss twins had been trying to build a website. Work had been progressing very slowly because none of them could program. Their plan was to make a dating and nightlife site called HarvardConnection. It would help people at Harvard find boyfriends or girlfriends, provide news about parties, and offer nightclub discounts.

Zuckerberg met with the Winkelvoss twins and Narendra on November 25, 2003. The three older students told him how important it was for their site to be the first to launch at Harvard. They asked Zuckerberg to finish programming their site. He said he would do the job in return for a share in the project. There was no contract and no payment.

Working on Thefacebook

Zuckerberg kept in touch with the Winkelvoss twins and Narendra to report on his progress. At first, he thought building HarvardConnection would be an easy job. "It seems like it shouldn't take too long to implement," he e-mailed on November 30. And on December 1, he mailed that "everything was working on his system."

Then the tone of Zuckerberg's e-mails

Tyler (R) and Cameron (L) Winklevoss asked Zuckerberg to help build their social network at Harvard

suddenly changed. He said he was too busy with his studies to work on HarvardConnection.

The truth was he had started to build his own social networking site.

Zuckerberg worked hard over the holidays at the end of December and the start of January. On January 11, 2004, he paid $35 to register the domain name Thefacebook.com. He had a meeting with the Winkelvoss twins and Narendra about HarvardConnection three days later on January 14, but he did not tell them about his own project.

The boy from Brazil

Although Zuckerberg had already produced many websites as a hobby, he was much more serious about Thefacebook. He asked his friend Eduardo Saverin to invest some money in the site and help him with the business side of things. Saverin was a Brazilian who had been to high school in Miami. Like Zuckerberg, he was Jewish. Saverin had made plenty of money working on Wall Street during the previous summer and was in the Harvard Investment Club. The two boys invested $1,000 each. They split the company: Zuckerberg had 70% and Saverin had 30%.

Part 2

The birth of Facebook

Thefacebook goes live

Zuckerberg launched Thefacebook.com on Wednesday, February 4, 2004. One of Zuckerberg's friends had created a logo for the site. It was a man's face covered with zeros and ones against a blue background. In fact, blue was the only color used in the site. Do you know why? It's because Zuckerberg is colorblind and cannot see red or green.

The text on the site said:

[Welcome to Thefacebook]

Thefacebook is an online directory that connects people through social networks at colleges.
   We have opened up Thefacebook for popular consumption at Harvard University.

Part 2 The birth of Facebook

You can use Thefacebook to

- Search for people at your school
- Find out who are in your classes
- See a visualization of your social network.

To get started, click below to register. If you have already registered, you can log in.

Thefacebook was an instant success. Over half of all Harvard's undergraduates joined in the first week. By the end of February, three-quarters of them were members. Students no longer said "e-mail me"; instead, they started to say "Facebook me."

So everybody was happy. Well no, not quite everybody. Narendra and the Winkelvoss twins learned about Thefacebook from an article in the February 9th issue of the Harvard student newspaper. They were shocked. Zuckerberg had been lying to them for weeks! He had stolen their idea! He had told them he was building their site when he'd actually been copying it!

The Winkelvoss brothers contacted their father, Howard Winkelvoss, a wealthy entrepreneur. Howard's lawyers sent a letter to Zuckerberg telling him to close down the site. The twins also complained to Lawrence Summers, the president of the university. Summers told them it was a problem for the law courts, not the university.

Zuckerberg always said that the two sites, Thefacebook and HarvardConnection, were completely different.

The social network boom

In fact, social networking was already booming before the Winkelvoss twins, Narendra, or Zuckerberg got interested in it. None of them invented the idea.

Friendster, the first really successful social networking site, had launched in March 2002. People used their real names and had profiles with photos. They joined by getting an invitation from another user. In this way, Friendster established the basic structure for a social network. Three million people joined Friendster in its first few months. But the site's success did not last long. There were too many visitors for the company's servers. Friendster quickly began to suffer from technical problems.

Tom Anderson and Chris DeWolfe, two digital entrepreneurs from Los Angeles, saw a business opportunity in Friendster's difficulties. They launched a rival social network called MySpace in August 2003. MySpace targeted young, trendy, creative people, musicians in particular. It soon became more popular than Friendster.

There were also social networks especially for colleges. Stanford University had its own social network starting in November 2001. Interestingly, the Stanford network was built by a Turkish student, Orkut Buyukkoten. After graduation, he went to work for Google where he built "Orkut," Google's first social network. Orkut actually launched in January 2004, two weeks before Thefacebook.

What is a "facebook"?

All American universities publish "facebooks." Facebooks are simple directories that list all the new students with basic information and a photograph. By 2003, many Harvard students, who had grown up with the Internet, thought that the university should put its facebooks online. The Harvard newspaper thought so, too. This was one of the topics that Zuckerberg and his math classmates discussed at their end-of-semester dinner in December 2003.

Some people think Zuckerberg got the idea for Thefacebook from the conversation at this dinner and not from the Winkelvoss twins. Two things are very clear: first, when he started building his website in December

2003, social networks were already very popular; second, many people at Harvard were already talking about creating an "online facebook for the whole university."

A talented roommate

On February 11, Thefacebook was one week old. Already, students at other colleges were contacting Zuckerberg. "Please can you bring Thefacebook to our campus?" they asked him.

Dustin Moskovitz, one of Zuckerberg's three roommates
(David McClure)

The site was growing too fast for Zuckerberg to do all the programming by himself. He had three roommates in his suite at Kirkland House, and he asked one of them, Dustin Moskovitz, to help him. Moskovitz was an economics major, but he bought a book and taught himself computer programming over a weekend.

Moskovitz was just a beginner. As a result, he could not program quickly, but he was willing to work long hours. In fact, Moskovitz worked so hard that the other boys nicknamed him "the ox." (Zuckerberg also described him as "a workaholic and a machine.") Moskovitz was so useful that Zuckerberg gave him 5% of the new company. Moskovitz later became chief technical officer, or CTO, of Facebook and—because he is one week younger than Zuckerberg—the world's youngest billionaire.

Moskovitz's first big job was helping Thefacebook expand to other schools. It was a boring job. To add a new school, he had to input lots of data like e-mail addresses, course lists, and dormitory names.

Going national

Thanks to Moskovitz's hard work, Thefacebook opened at Columbia (New York) on February 25, at Stanford (California) on February 26 and Yale (Connecticut) on February 29. Why did Zuckerberg choose these three schools? Because they already had their own successful online social networks and Zuckerberg wanted Thefacebook to be No. 1 not just at Harvard but at colleges all over the country.

Expansion continues

Thefacebook was a success wherever it went. In March, the site was launched at seven more of America's top universities: Dartmouth, Cornell, MIT, University of Pennsylvania, Princeton, Brown and Boston University. At Dartmouth, 42.5% of all the students joined on the first day.

By the end of March, Thefacebook had more than 30,000 users. Originally, users could only contact (or "friend") people from their own university, but now Zuckerberg and Moskovitz made it possible for students to contact their friends at different universities.

The poet of Thefacebook

As Thefacebook opened on more campuses, journalists from student newspapers around the country wanted to interview Mark Zuckerberg, its founder. He was too shy and too busy to do interviews, so he hired Chris Hughes, another of his roommates, to be Thefacebook's official spokesman.

Hughes was a good-looking young man with

Chris Hughes, Thefacebook's official spokesman (USV)

blue eyes and blond hair. Like Zuckerberg, Hughes was a graduate of Phillips Exeter. (His family was not rich, so he went there on a scholarship.) But unlike Zuckerberg, Moskovitz, or Saverin, Hughes was not interested in programming, economics, or business.

Hughes was majoring in French history and literature. This gave him a different viewpoint from that of the other boys. He was good at guessing how people might want to connect with one another online. He knew how people would feel about things. That's why his roommates nicknamed him "the Empath."

Hughes worked for Facebook until January 2007. He left the company to help an Illinois senator named Barack Obama campaign for the Democratic nomination and then for the presidency.

Zuckerberg was certainly very lucky to have talented roommates like Hughes and Moskovitz.

Thefacebook becomes a company

When Zuckerberg launched Thefacebook, he had rented one computer server for $85 a month. As the number of users increased, the company needed more servers. By the end of March, Thefacebook was renting five servers. Server rental was now costing over $400 per month.

The company needed more money. Zuckerberg and Saverin each invested another $10,000. How did two young students have so much money? Zuckerberg had earned a lot from programming jobs, while Saverin had made $300,000 on the futures market during the 2003 summer break.

In April 2004, Saverin established Thefacebook as a limited liability company (LLC) in Florida, the state where he had been to high school. April was also when Saverin started trying to sell advertising on the site. They needed income.

The advertising problem

In May, Saverin teamed up with a company called Y2M, a firm that specialized in selling advertisements for college newspapers. Thanks to Y2M, Thefacebook got an advertisement from Mastercard, the credit card company. "We want to advertise on Thefacebook for four months," said Mastercard.

On the first day of the advertising campaign, the people at Mastercard got a big surprise. They got more applications in one day than they had expected to get in the whole four months! Y2M was very impressed. They asked to invest in Thefacebook. Zuckerberg was not interested. "No thanks," he said. "We're going to change the world."

Zuckerberg was much more interested in creating a "good user experience" than in getting advertisements. And as he owned the company, he could do whatever he wanted.

He refused to accept advertisements from "boring" companies like the investment bank Goldman Sachs. Sometimes he also added text underneath advertisements on his site. "We don't like these advertisements but they help pay the bills," the message said.

Go West, young man

Zuckerberg decided to rent a house for Thefacebook team in Palo Alto, California, for the 2004 summer holidays. Zuckerberg chose Palo Alto because it was "where all the tech giants came from."

Dustin Moskovitz, Adam D'Angelo (Zuckerberg's friend from Phillips Exeter and the co-creator of Synapse who was studying at the California Institute of Technology), and Andrew McCollum, the Harvard student who had designed Thefacebook logo, went with Zuckerberg to California.

Chris Hughes, the official spokesman, had

to go to France to study. Eduardo Saverin went to New York to work in an investment firm—and to try to sell more advertisements for Thefacebook.

Bad boy hero

There was one other reason that Zuckerberg had rented a house in California. He wanted to be near his hacker hero, Sean Parker.

Sean Parker was a legend in the computer world. He had started programming when he was seven. He had been arrested by the FBI for hacking when he was sixteen. In 1999, aged just nineteen, he had co-founded Napster, a popular music file-sharing service. (The record companies eventually shut Napster down.) Then, in November 2002, at

Sean Parker, a legend in the computer world (Andrew Mager)

the age of twenty-two, Parker had launched Plaxo, an online address book and social networking site.

In March 2004, Parker saw Thefacebook on the computer of a friend at Stanford. He immediately e-mailed Zuckerberg to ask to meet him. Parker had a good sixth sense. He could tell in advance what technology trends were going to become popular. And he was certain that social networking was going to be "the next big thing." He promised to introduce Zuckerberg to investors and to the managers of other social networking sites like Friendster and LinkedIn.

In April, Parker flew to New York to have dinner with Zuckerberg, Saverin, and their girlfriends. They met at a trendy Chinese restaurant. Nobody except Parker or Zuckerberg got the chance to speak. Zuckerberg talked about his dreams of "building something with long-term cultural value" and of "taking over the world." Parker was impressed.

Sean Parker in the house

That summer, Zuckerberg and Parker met again by chance in the street in Palo Alto. Parker was just moving out of his rented house. When they went out to dinner that night, Parker explained that he had nowhere to live and not much money. Zuckerberg invited him to live with them in Thefacebook house.

In the house, the boys always got out of bed late and did their programming wearing their pajamas. When there was an important project to do, Zuckerberg would not let anyone leave the house. "We're in lockdown!" he used to shout. "Nobody leaves until we're finished."

Moskovitz, Zuckerberg, and Parker made a good team. Each of them was good at something different. Moskovitz worked on managing the site. Zuckerberg thought about its future direction. And Parker, who had the experience of founding two companies, thought about Thefacebook as a business.

The boys did not work all the time. They used Thefacebook to invite girls from nearby Stanford to parties where they played drinking games. They also swam in the pool, watched movies, and played computer games.

Building a businesslike business

While Zuckerberg and his friends worked on the site, Parker started talking to investors. Thefacebook was obviously going to need some money soon. The site was made with open source software, which was free, but other things cost money. Zuckerberg was paying his friends' salaries. Running servers for 100,000 users was also not cheap.

They knew they would get more new members when school started again in September, so over the summer, they upgraded their database and their servers. They didn't want any technical problems to damage their reputation as had happened with Friendster.

Parker vs. Saverin

Parker hired a lawyer to restructure the fast-growing company. But back in New York, Eduardo Saverin was not happy about Parker's growing power. He wrote a note to Zuckerberg. "Please send me a letter to confirm that I, not Sean Parker, am in charge of the business," it said. "If you won't confirm that I control the business, I will use my 30% share to stop the company from getting money from investors."

With his business background, Saverin believed that selling advertisements—his job—was the most important thing for Thefacebook.

Nobody in Palo Alto agreed. First, they thought that advertisements were ugly. Second, they thought that the important thing was to create an appealing site that attracted lots of users. As the site got more and more successful, advertisements would start coming in automatically.

Saverin's counterattack fails

Parker and his lawyer made a new company structure for Thefacebook. Now Zuckerberg had 51% of the business, Saverin 34.5%, and Moskovitz and Parker about 7.5% each.

Parker wanted to push Saverin out because he had refused to come to California and work with them. He told Saverin that when new people invested in Thefacebook, his 34% share of the company would go down.

Saverin was shocked and angry. He froze the company bank account in Florida. As usual, Thefacebook needed to buy new servers, but now it couldn't pay its bills! Over the summer, Zuckerberg and his family invested $85,000 to keep the company running smoothly. (Zuckerberg later repaid his father by giving him 2 million shares.)

By the end of the holidays, Thefacebook had more than 200,000 users. Zuckerberg and Moskovitz decided not to go back to Harvard. (Almost thirty years earlier, another very famous computer entrepreneur had also dropped out of Harvard. His name was Bill Gates.) They planned to stay in Palo Alto and expand Thefacebook to 70 more universities. Meanwhile, Hughes, D'Angelo, and Saverin all went back to school.

Part 3

---✶---

Becoming a real company

Thefacebook's first investor

Thefacebook had to have money to buy more servers for its 200,000 users. The company needed to find an investor fast. Parker asked Reid Hoffman, the founder of LinkedIn, the business networking site, if he wanted to invest.

Hoffman recommended his friend Peter Thiel. Hoffman and Thiel had worked together at PayPal, the online payment company. When eBay, the online auction company, bought PayPal in 2002, Thiel, the co-founder and CEO, became very rich. He used his money to set up Clarium Capital, a fund to invest in tech ventures.

When the boys went to Clarium, it was Parker who made the presentation. "Thefacebook is still small. That's because you can only get it in certain schools," he explained. "But when Thefacebook opens at a new school, almost all the students join, and almost all of them visit the site every day."

Thiel agreed to invest $500,000 for 10% of the company. He also became a director of Thefacebook. Parker and Zuckerberg trusted Thiel because, like them, he had been a successful Internet entrepreneur. Thiel's advice to Zuckerberg was very simple. "Don't fuck it up," he said.

Parker had lost his job at the two companies he had founded, Napster and Plaxo, because investors did not like his wild, bad-boy lifestyle. Parker wanted to make sure that no investor could push Zuckerberg out. He therefore created a special structure. Thefacebook had three directors—Parker, Thiel and Zuckerberg—but Zuckerberg controlled two seats on the board. "I wanted to protect Mark," said Parker.

One million users

Zuckerberg and Moskovitz began adding new features to the site like the Wall and Groups. They also started expanding from the elite Ivy League to more ordinary universities like the University of Oklahoma. They could now add new schools easily because they had automated the whole process.

Thefacebook was also starting to earn more money from advertising. It created a special group page for Paramount Pictures' "The SpongeBob SquarePants Movie." Apple also started a group for fans of its computers. Apple paid a minimum of $50,000 per month.

Money was coming in, but costs were rising. As well as renting servers, the young company had to pay $20,000 a month to lawyers. The Winkelvoss twins and Narendra had accused Zuckerberg of stealing their idea, and he was fighting back.

Despite these problems, the company kept

on growing. In September 2004, membership doubled from 200,000 to 400,000. It was 500,000 by October 21, and on November 30, just ten months after launch, Thefacebook hit one million users. There was a big party at Frisson, a nightclub that Peter Thiel owned in San Francisco.

Playing tricks on VCs

As Thefacebook grew bigger, more and more venture capital firms—or VCs—wanted to invest in it. One of the most famous VCs was a firm called Sequoia Capital. Founded in 1972, Sequoia had invested in giant companies like Apple, Oracle, and Yahoo!.

Sequoia had also invested in Plaxo, Parker's most recent business. Eventually, however, Sequoia had pushed him out of his own company. Parker decided to use Zuckerberg to get his revenge. He set up a meeting for Zuckerberg at Sequoia at 8:00 AM.

On the day of the presentation, Zuckerberg was late. He arrived at the Sequoia office wearing a T-shirt and pajama pants. "Sorry, I overslept," he said. Sequoia really wanted to invest in Thefacebook, but instead, Zuckerberg talked about Wirehog, a software program he had made for sharing text, video and photos.

Zuckerberg's presentation was called "The Top Ten Reasons You Should Not Invest in Wirehog." The reasons included "because Sean Parker is involved" and "because we arrived late in our pajamas."

Later Zuckerberg was embarrassed about his rude and silly behavior. Of course, he was only twenty years old at the time.

Lessons from the Washington Post

One company that Zuckerberg treated with more respect was the Washington Post. Christopher Ma, the man in charge of new media

PART 3 BECOMING A REAL COMPANY

development at the Washington Post, had heard about Thefacebook from his daughter at Harvard. He invited Zuckerberg and Parker to the company's head office in Washington to talk about investing in their firm.

Don Graham, the Washington Post CEO, also came to the meeting. Graham got a very positive impression of Zuckerberg. He thought Thefacebook was "one of the best ideas he'd ever heard."

Graham warned Zuckerberg that venture capital companies only wanted short-term profits. The Washington Post, however, was different. "If we invest in Thefacebook, it will be a long-term thing," said Graham. "We won't put pressure on you."

Zuckerberg liked Graham and he liked the idea of the Washington Post investing in his company. Graham's company offered to pay $6 million for 10% of Thefacebook. But plenty of other firms were keen to invest in the Thefacebook too.

Competition to invest

Parker was the showman who made the presentations to investors. "Thefacebook has 2 million users at 370 schools," he used to say. "65% of our users visit the site every day. On some days, our membership grows by 3% per day."

Viacom, a media group that owns Paramount Pictures and many TV stations, offered to buy Thefacebook for $75 million. Viacom wanted to combine Thefacebook with MTV, its music television channel, as they both appealed to young people.

But there was another company that wanted to invest in Thefacebook even more: an investment firm called Accel Partners. In the 1990s, Accel had made lots of money investing in Macromedia, the creator of Flash and Dreamweaver software, and Real Networks, which made compressed audio and video formats.

Part 3 Becoming a real company

Four year had passed since the 2001 dot-com crash. Accel now had $400 million to invest. "Find me an Internet company that could grow very big," Jim Breyer, a director of Accel, told the young Kevin Efrusy. (Efrusy had joined the firm only two years ago.)

Efrusy had missed a chance to invest in Flickr, the photo-sharing site. This time he really wanted to succeed. On Friday, April 1, he met Parker and Zuckerberg at Thefacebook office. After listening to their presentation, Efrusy promised to make an offer on Monday.

A big deal

Over the weekend, Efrusy went to Stanford to do some market research. He asked the students on campus about Thefacebook. They all said they were "addicted" to it. Efrusy offered to invest $10 million, valuing Thefacebook at $80 million. That was 30%

more than the Washington Post's offer!

Parker liked the Accel offer—it was more money!—but Zuckerberg was not sure. On Tuesday night, Accel invited Thefacebook staff to dinner at an expensive restaurant to celebrate their deal. In the middle of the dinner, Zuckerberg went to the bathroom—and didn't come back out. One of Thefacebook managers went to see what was happening. Zuckerberg was sitting on the bathroom floor, crying, "I can't do this deal," he said. "I made a promise to Don Graham at the Washington Post."

"Well, why don't you call Graham tomorrow and talk to him," the manager suggested. Graham was disappointed not to get the deal, but he was impressed that Zuckerberg had phoned him. "Mark, don't worry," he said. "Take Accel's money and good luck growing your company."

On Wednesday morning, Zuckerberg went to see Breyer in the Accel office. He got Accel to increase their offer. Finally, they invested

$12.7 million for 14% of the company, valuing Thefacebook at $98 million. Breyer also became a director.

As a result of the deal with Accel, Eduardo Saverin's share of the company fell from 34% to less than 10%. Saverin was angry. He stopped working for the company completely. Moskovitz, Zuckerberg, and Parker—who all had salaries of $65,000 a year—each got a cash bonus of $1 million each.

That night, Zuckerberg went to a gas station to fill his car. A crazy young man carrying a gun came toward him. "Give me your money," he shouted. Zuckerberg took a risk. Paying no attention, he climbed into his car and drove away. Nothing happened.

Zuckerberg was a truly lucky young man!

Thefacebook grows up

Thefacebook now had millions of dollars in the bank. The company was ready to expand even faster. To do that, it needed to hire good, experienced managers. The trouble was that older managers did not want to work with a gang of crazy 20-year-olds. (Remember, most of Thefacebook staff were self-taught programmers who had dropped out of college and liked to work at night.)

Older managers weren't sure if social networks were just a short-lived boom or were going to be popular in the long-term. They weren't sure if Thefacebook, which was still only for college students, could really grow into a big company that appealed to everyone.

Accel told Zuckerberg to "behave more like a leader." Zuckerberg moved out of the company house. He stopped writing software and started focusing more on strategy. He also started studying management and "shadowed" Don Graham at the Washington Post for four days to learn about leadership.

While Zuckerberg became more grown-up, the rest of the company remained young and crazy. "We wanted to be Silicon Valley's

PART 3 BECOMING A REAL COMPANY

Graffiti-style artwork on the walls of Facebook headquarters creates a fun atmosphere (EPA=時事)

coolest company," Parker said. "We wanted to be a fun, rock'n'roll place to work."

As part of this cool image, Parker hired David Choe, a graffiti artist to decorate the offices with wild, colorful paintings. (Choe was paid in shares, not cash. By 2012, his shares were worth $200 million!) Most of the staff (but not Zuckerberg) lived together in rented houses and had crazy parties at the weekend.

Social networks are serious business

In July 2005, News Corporation, a huge media company, paid $580 million to buy MySpace. (With 21 million users, MySpace was about seven times bigger than Thefacebook.) Zuckerberg, however, was not interested in selling. "I spend my time thinking how to build this business, not how to exit it," he said.

Although it was still much smaller than MySpace, Thefacebook was growing fast, expanding from three million members in June 2005 to five million by October. Zuckerberg was also starting to "think big." He wanted Thefacebook to become a "utility" like a telephone, water, or electricity company. He wanted to create a service that anybody (not just students) could use anywhere.

This "utility" concept explains why Thefacebook always had a very simple white design. The site itself was not important. The point was for users to have relationships with other users. The company also made its name simpler, changing "Thefacebook" to "Facebook." That was Sean Parker's idea.

Goodbye, Sean Parker

Changing the company name was the last thing Parker did at Facebook.

At the end of August, Parker went to the seaside in North Carolina to kitesurf. He was having a party in the house he had rented when the police came in. (The neighbors had complained about the noise.) There were two problems. First, one of the guests was a girl from Facebook who was under the legal drinking age. Second, there was cocaine in the house.

Accel Partners said that Parker should leave the company. Napster, Plaxo, and now Facebook: this was the third time Parker had been pushed out of a company. Despite losing his job, Parker and Zuckerberg remain friends. Parker still gives business advice to Zuckerberg even now.

Photo-hosting and tagging

In fall 2005, Zuckerberg decided to open the site to the 37,000 high schools in the United States. By April 2006, Facebook had over one million high school users!

Another big success at this time was adding photo-hosting to the site. The big question was how Facebook could host photos in a different way from other websites. Facebook staff discussed the problem. They decided that the thing people cared about most was who was in a photo. So they made it possible for users to "tag" (add a name tag to) people in their photos. Tagging photos was so popular that in a few years, Facebook had become the world's No. 1 photo site. By 2012, 300 million photographs were uploaded to

Facebook every day!

The photo-hosting experience taught people at Facebook an important lesson. A simple service became special when it was linked to people's relationships.

More management problems

Big media companies were still interested in buying Facebook. Zuckerberg and his executives spent a lot of time talking to firms like TimeWarner, Yahoo!, and Viacom (who offered $1.5 billion for the company). The Facebook staff, however, were unhappy. They didn't know what was going on. Was Facebook going to be sold? Was it going to stay independent?

Zuckerberg was still young. The main reason he was meeting all these people from different companies was to learn about the media business from them. He never planned to sell his company. When he realized the meetings were upsetting the staff, he stopped having them. He hired an executive coach to teach him how to be a better CEO. He started having more face-to-face meetings with his managers and "town-hall meetings" with all the staff.

Failures and successes

In May 2006, Facebook launched a new service. It was called "Work Networks." It was designed to help people who worked together stay in touch. The service was not a success (except for inside the U.S. Army). Zuckerberg was worried. Did Work Networks' failure mean that adults were not interested in Facebook? Would Facebook never be able to expand out of universities and high schools?

The company was now having more success in advertising. Because Facebook users posted information on what sex they were, how old they were, where they lived, what music they liked, and so on, it was easy for companies to target advertisements accurately.

In 2005, when singer Gwen Stefani released a song with a cheerleader chant chorus, Facebook was able to promote it just to cheerleaders. When Chase Manhattan Bank created a special credit card for students in 2006, they set up a group page on Facebook. 34,000 students joined the group in one week!

In June 2006, Interpublic, one of the world's "big four" advertising agencies, made a deal to spend $10 million that year on Facebook. (They also bought 0.5% of the stock.) The advertising world was starting to see potential in Facebook.

Open Registrations and News Feed

Facebook made two important changes in late 2006. First, it launched a new service called News Feed to tell you what your friends were doing. Second, it allowed "open registrations." That meant that anybody—not just university or high-school students—could join.

Facebook turned on NewsFeed on September 5, 2006. Some users didn't like it because it automatically told your Facebook friends what you were doing. (That's called "push" communication.) They started calling Facebook "Stalkerbook."

When Zuckerberg saw how many users were unhappy, he quickly changed the privacy settings and published a letter to say sorry. "We really messed this up," the letter said.

This often happened at Facebook. A new service was introduced. Users complained about the impact on privacy. Zuckerberg said sorry, made some small changes—and the service ended up becoming popular.

On September 26, 2006, Facebook switched to open registration. Now anybody could join the site. At the beginning it wasn't clear if adults liked Facebook as much as young people. But Zuckerberg didn't need to worry. After two weeks, the number of people joining Facebook had risen from 20,000 to 50,000 every day. Open registration was a big success!

The Platform Strategy

Ever since launching Facebook, Zuckerberg had dreamed of making Facebook into a "platform." A "platform" means an environment where other software applications can run. Microsoft Windows, Apple iOS, or Google Android are all examples of platforms.

Making Facebook into a platform would make it more attractive to users. They could use Facebook not just to keep in touch with friends but to play games or share news articles with them. Being a platform is a good way to get user loyalty and establish a strong market position. Zuckerberg believed that his platform strategy would make Facebook bigger than MySpace.

Work on building an application programming interface (API) started in August 2006, and it was launched on May 27, 2007. Zuckerberg made a presentation. "Together we are starting a movement," he said to the crowd. Then he showed them applications by the *Washington Post* newspaper and Microsoft.

The platform strategy was a big success. Thousands of developers created applications, or apps, to run on Facebook. The most famous Facebook apps are probably the social games made by Zynga.

Zynga started out by creating a poker game for Facebook. This was not especially successful. But games like FarmVille (managing a fantasy farm) and CityVille (building a fantasy city) were huge hits. By the time Zynga went public in December 2011, it was worth $7 billion.

One year after opening up Facebook to adults, half of its 50 million users were based outside the United States. As usual, the company needed money for hardware, so it sold a 1.6% share to Microsoft for $240 million. (Microsoft also managed the advertisements on Facebook in the U.S. and overseas.)

The Beacon disaster

On November 6, 2007, Facebook held a big event for advertisers. Zuckerberg introduced a new service called Beacon. When a user bought something online, Beacon would send a message to his friends like "John rented 'Pirates of the Caribbean' at Netflix" or "Claude bought a pair of Nike sneakers at Zappos."

Zuckerberg was very proud of Beacon. "Once every hundred years, media changes," he said at the presentation. "Before it was the mass media, now people will share information among their own connections. Nothing influences people more than a recommendation from a friend."

But Facebook users hated Beacon. How

could you buy a surprise present for someone if Facebook told them you had bought it? The media wrote many negative articles about Facebook not respecting people's privacy.

Beacon was a public relations disaster. Worse still, for three weeks, Zuckerberg did nothing in response. Then, at the beginning of December, he finally said sorry on The Facebook Blog. "We've made a lot of mistakes building this feature," he wrote. "But we've made even more with how we've handled them. We simply did a bad job with this release, and I apologize for it."

Facebook had damaged its own image. For several months, fewer people joined the site. Beacon was eventually shut down in 2009.

Some of the new product ideas were much more successful. Facebook Connect, which was launched in May 2008, is one example. Facebook Connect enables users to log in to other sites with their Facebook identity. You can use it for commenting on a news story, for example. Because your Facebook identity is your real identity, it keeps online discussions polite.

Part 4

A giant of the Internet

The coming of Sheryl Sandberg

Nearly all of the powerful people in Silicon Valley are men. But there is one big exception: Sheryl Sandberg. Sandberg started out working as chief of staff to Lawrence Summers, treasury secretary for President Bill Clinton. She joined Google in 2001 (when the company was three years old) and built its advertising business to an enormous size.

Zuckerberg met Sandberg at a Christmas party in December 2008. After seven years, she was interested in leaving Google—and Zuckerberg was interested in hiring her. Sandberg knew a lot about making money from online advertising, and she had experience in government. (With privacy problems becoming an issue, the government was more and more interested in Internet companies like Facebook.)

Zuckerberg interviewed Sandberg many times. He wanted to be sure she was right for Facebook. After all, she was a 39-year-old woman joining a company full of 20-year-old boys! Sandberg eventually joined Facebook in March 2008.

The Sandberg effect

After Sandberg joined the company, Zuckerberg immediately took a long holiday. He went backpacking in Germany, Turkey, Japan, and India (where he visited the that ashram Apple's Steve Jobs had gone to in the 1970s). While Zuckerberg was away, Sandberg had long meetings with the management team. They discussed how to earn more money from advertising ("monetize the site").

Sandberg and her colleagues decided that there were two kinds of advertisements: advertisements that "fulfill demand" and advertisements that "generate demand." Google ads help people find things they are already interested in and searching for, so Google ads "fulfill" existing demand. But ads on Facebook were different. They were more like TV ads which "generate" demand and get people interested in something new.

Sandberg talked to Zuckerberg when he came back from his trip. "I don't want silly advertisements that annoy people," he said. Finally he and Sandberg decided that Facebook would host "engagement ads." In an engagement ad, the advertiser invites people to do something. One ice cream company, for example, asked its Facebook fans to choose the company's new flavor of ice cream.

As the company got bigger, some of the original Facebook founders started to leave. Chris Hughes had left Facebook in January 2007. Dustin Moskovitz, the CTO who had also been Zuckerberg's roommate, left in 2008. He started a new company, Asana, that helps teams coordinate projects online.

Part 4 A giant of the Internet

Adam D'Angelo left in 2008 to set up Quora, a question-and-answer website. Charlie Cheever, the creator of Facebook Connect, left with him.

They left for several reasons: the company was too big; they didn't like the focus on money; they no longer felt close to their old friend Zuckerberg. Some people also thought that Sheryl Sandberg had too much power. People said that if you were not a FOSS ("friend of Sheryl Sandberg") life at Facebook could be difficult.

By 2011, advertising accounted for 85% of Facebook's revenue. Just as at Google, Sandberg had turned Facebook into a hugely successful business. That is probably why Sandberg was paid $30.9 million—more than 20 times as much as Mark Zuckerberg himself—that year.

Facebook in other languages

At the start of 2008, Zuckerberg decided that Facebook should be available in other languages besides English. Instead of hiring a translation company to translate the site, Zuckerberg decided to use "crowd sourcing." He asked Facebook users to translate the site into their own language.

The first language was Spanish (January), followed by German and French (March). Four thousand users needed just two days to create the French version. By December 2011, Facebook was available in over 70 languages, and 80% of users were outside North America.

Facebook and global politics

Facebook was not equally successful in all countries. In Brazil, Orkut, Google's first social network, remains more popular. In Japan, Mixi is very strong; in Russia there is vKontakte and in Korea, Cyworld. Meanwhile China banned Facebook on June 4, 2009, the 20th anniversary of the Tiananmen Square massacre.

The Chinese government was afraid of Facebook. Why? Because Facebook gave ordinary people the chance to express themselves and organize movements. In one famous example, a man in Colombia set up a Facebook group to protest against a terrorist group, the Revolutionary Armed Forces of Colombia, or FARC. He called his group "One Million Voices Against FARC."

The anti-FARC group page opened on January 4, 2008. One month later, on March 4, 10 million people marched against FARC in the cities of Colombia, not to mention two million more elsewhere in the world. Facebook meant real people power.

A similar thing happened in 2009 in Iran. When the challenger, Mir Hossein Mousavi, unfairly lost the election, he used Facebook to tell his supporters to go onto the streets and protest. Facebook was also important in the uprising in Egypt in 2011. Many people used the expression "The Facebook revolution" to describe the uprising that pushed Hosni Mubarak from power.

Zuckerberg believed in the positive political power of Facebook. "When everyone can express their opinion quickly, you get a better governed world and a fairer world," he said.

Fighting the Winkelvosses

The Winkelvosses had finally launched their website in spring 2004, changing its name from Harvard Connection to ConnectU. In fall 2004, using the lawyers of their rich father, they officially accused Zuckerberg of stealing their idea of creating the first niche social network for college students at Harvard and then expanding to other colleges.

The case was settled in mid-2008. Many of the details are secret, but it is believed that Facebook paid $65 million to the Winkelvosses and Narendra. This included buying their unsuccessful website, ConnectU, and shutting it down.

None of the three showed much entrepreneurial ability after leaving Harvard. They all went to business school. Narendra set up SumZero, a network for professional investors. Cameron Winkelvoss runs a website called Guest of a Guest, a blog about parties in posh U.S. towns and cities. He and his brother Tyler also appeared in an advertisement for a brand of pistachio nuts.

Well-timed publicity

On September 24, 2010, Zuckerberg appeared on the Oprah Winfrey show, the most popular TV talk show in the U.S. He announced that he was going to give $100 million to schools in Newark, New Jersey. (Newark's school system is very bad.)

Oprah asked him why he was giving so much money to schools. "Every child deserves a good education," Zuckerberg answered. "Right now that's not happening. I've had a lot of opportunities in my life, and a lot of that comes from having gone to really good schools. I want to make sure everyone has those same opportunities."

Some people didn't believe Zuckerberg. They thought he was giving the money to create good publicity. Why did he need good publicity just then? It was because a new movie about Facebook was coming out the next week. Called *The Social Network*, it painted a very negative picture of Zuckerberg.

The Social Network movie

The Social Network opened in almost 2,800 theaters in the United States on October 1,

Part 4 A giant of the Internet

2010. It was No. 1 at the U.S. box office for two weekends in a row. It later won three Academy Awards and earned almost $225 million worldwide.

The director was David Fincher, famous for tough, clever thrillers like *Seven* (1995) and *Fight Club* (1999). The writer was Aaron Sorkin, creator of *The West Wing* (1999–2006), a political drama about the staff of the White House. Critics loved the movie: "a high IQ movie," said *Time* magazine; "brilliantly entertaining," said *The New Yorker*.

The movie's tagline was: "You don't get to 500 million friends without making a few enemies." (500 million was the number of Facebook users when the movie came out.) The movie presents Zuckerberg as a very unpleasant person: angry, arrogant, dishonest, and disloyal.

In the movie, Zuckerberg cannot get a girlfriend. He is angry that he cannot get into the historic fraternities at Harvard because he is Jewish. He steals the idea for his social media site from the Winkelvosses and Narendra. He cheats his co-founder Eduardo Saverin out of his share of the business.

The movie had a very clear message: despite all his money and success, Mark Zuckerberg was a sad and lonely man.

Truth or fiction?

Zuckerberg was not happy about *The Social Network*. "I wish that nobody had made a movie about me while I was still alive," he told Oprah. His real life was much less dramatic than the movie. "I spent the past six years working hard and coding Facebook," he explained.

There was one part of the movie that was accurate: his clothes. "It's interesting the stuff they focused on getting right. Every single shirt or fleece they had in that movie is actually a shirt or fleece that I own," he commented.

Why was the movie so negative? Why was Zuckerberg the villain and Eduardo Saverin the hero? It's mainly because the movie was based on a book called *The Accidental Billionaires: The Founding of Facebook* by Ben Mezrich. When Mezrich was writing his book, he only spoke to one person from Facebook: Eduardo Saverin.

Parker and Zuckerberg had pushed Saverin out of the company. Of course Saverin was angry. That's why he presented a negative picture of his old colleagues.

Did the movie damage the image of Facebook? Probably not. In a way, it was like a $40 million global advertising campaign— paid for by Hollywood. Indeed in December 2010, two months after the movie came out, *Time* magazine named Zuckerberg its "person of the year."

"For connecting more than half a billion people and mapping the social relations among them, for creating a new system of exchanging information and for changing how we live our lives, Mark Elliot Zuckerberg is TIME's 2010 Person of the Year," said the magazine.

Taking over the world

Facebook just kept on getting more and more popular. By June 2011, it had 750 million members; by September 2011, it had 800 million; and by February 2012, it had 845 million members.

There were two key reasons Facebook continued growing: one was the "network effect." The more people joined Facebook, the better the experience became for all users, so more and more people continued to join. The other reason was that Facebook continued evolving.

For example, when the micro-blog Twitter became very popular, Zuckerberg added a "What's on your mind?" box where you could post your thoughts. He also teamed

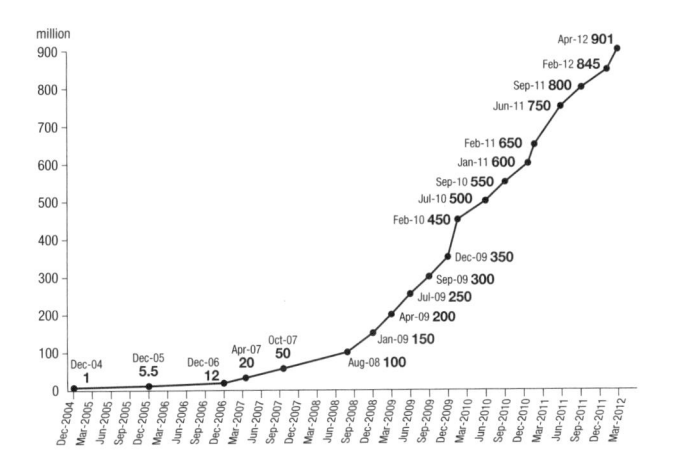

Facebook users in millions
(Source: Ben Foster and Facebook)

up with Skype to offer free phone calls inside Facebook.

In December 2011, he launched Timeline where you show your whole life story online. "Timeline is the heart of your Facebook experience, completely rethought from the ground up," said Zuckerberg at the presentation. "Timeline is a new way to express who you are."

A more human Internet

Zuckerberg strongly believed that the Facebook version of the Internet was better than the Google version of the Internet. Why? Because in the Google Internet the computer controls the experience, while the Facebook Internet is based on people's relationships ("the social graph") and people's activities ("the social stream"). Basically, the Facebook Internet is a more human Internet.

Zuckerberg was ambitious. His goal, he said, was "to turn Facebook into a worldwide platform where you can type in anyone's name, find the person you're looking for and communicate with them."

Floating on the stock market

By 2012, Zuckerberg had realized his ambitious goal. Along with Apple, Amazon and

Part 4 A giant of the Internet

Google, Facebook was now one of the four "GAFA" companies controlling the Internet. It had 3,200 staff, revenues of $3.7 billion, profits of $1 billion, and 901 million users (and 488 million users of Facebook mobile).

In February 2012, Facebook announced that it would debut on the stock market.

Mark Zuckerberg was the biggest shareholder with 28.4% of the company. Then came Accel Partners with 11.4%. Moskovitz had 7.6%, Eduardo Saverin 5%, Sean Parker 4% and Peter Thiel 2.5%. Other Facebook staff owned a total of 30% of the company. Interestingly, Bono, the lead singer of supergroup U2, owned 1.5%.

The documents that Facebook published before its stock market debut included a letter written by Mark Zuckerberg. In the letter he writes about two important things: the mission of Facebook and Facebook's unusually open and flexible corporate culture.

Let's have a look at it.

The mission of Facebook

The letter opens with a description of the philosophy behind Facebook. The language is simple, but the thinking is very bold. Zuckerberg's main point is that his company was never just about making money. Through Facebook, he wanted to change the world.

> *Facebook was not originally created to be a company. It was built to accomplish a social mission—to make the world more open and connected.*
>
> *At Facebook, we're inspired by technologies that have revolutionized how people spread and consume information. Inventions like the printing press and the television led to a complete transformation of many important parts of society. They gave people a voice. They encouraged progress. They changed the way society was organized. They brought us closer together.*
>
> *Today, our society has reached another*

tipping point. We live at a moment when the majority of people in the world have access to the Internet or mobile phones—the tools necessary to start sharing what they're thinking, feeling and doing with whomever they want. Facebook hopes to build the services that give people the power to share and help them once again transform many of our institutions and industries.

We hope to strengthen how people relate to each other.

We hope to improve how people connect to businesses and the economy.

We hope to change how people relate to their governments and social institutions.

We don't build services to make money; we make money to build better services.

We think this is a good way to build something. These days I think more and more people want to use services from companies that believe in something beyond simply maximizing profits.

"The Hacker Way": Facebook's Corporate Culture

The letter continues with an interesting description of Facebook's unique culture. It shows how hard Facebook concentrates on being open and flexible so it can adapt to an ever-changing world.

> *At Facebook we have cultivated a unique culture and management approach that we call the Hacker Way. The word "hacker" usually has a negative meaning of "someone who breaks into computers." This is unfair. In reality, hacking just means building something quickly or testing the boundaries of what's possible. The majority of hackers I've met are people who want to have a positive impact on the world.*
>
> *The Hacker Way involves continuous improvement. Hackers believe that something can always be better, and that nothing is ever complete. They just have to go fix it.*

Part 4 A giant of the Internet

Hackers try to build the best services over the long term by quickly releasing and learning from smaller developments rather than trying to get everything right all at once.

Hacking is also a hands-on and active discipline. Instead of debating for days whether a new idea is possible or what the best way to build something is, hackers just prototype something and see what works.

Hacker culture is extremely open and meritocratic. Hackers believe that the best idea and implementation should always win — not the person who is best at lobbying for an idea or the person who manages the most people.

To encourage this approach, every few months we have a "hackathon," where everyone builds prototypes for new ideas they have. Many of our most successful products came out of hackathons, including Timeline, chat, video, our mobile development framework.

Facebook's Five Core Values

The letter then goes on to list Facebook's five core values.

> *Focus on Impact: Make sure we always focus on solving the most important problems.*
>
> *Move Fast: As companies grow, they slow down because they become afraid of making mistakes. Moving fast enables us to build more things and learn faster.*
>
> *Be Bold: In a world that's changing so quickly, you're guaranteed to fail if you don't take risks. We encourage everyone to make bold decisions, even if that means being wrong some of the time.*
>
> *Be Open: We make sure everyone at Facebook has access to as much information as possible about the company so they can make the best decisions and have the greatest impact.*
>
> *Build Social Value: Facebook exists to make the world more open and connected. We expect everyone at Facebook to focus every*

day on how to build real value for the world in everything they do.

There is a lot that older, more conservative companies can learn from Zuckerberg's management philosophy.

A giant deal on the way to a stock market listing

In early April 2012, Facebook announced that it was going to pay $1 billion to buy Instagram, an online photo-sharing iPhone application (or "app") with 27 million users. The price was extraordinarily high. After all, Instagram was only 18 months old, had just 13 employees, and had been valued at $500 million—or half of what Facebook paid—just one week before the deal.

But Instagram had something that Facebook did not. Designed from the start as a mobile app, Instagram was fast, fun, and much simpler to use than Facebook (which was designed for PCs). Technology is a fast-changing business. More and more people were using smartphones—not PCs—to interact with their friends online. Clearly Zuckerberg hoped that buying Instagram would give Facebook a strong foothold in the new world of iPhone and Android mobile apps and keep his company firmly in the front line.

The $1.00 man

Starting January 1, 2013, Mark Zuckerberg's salary will be reduced to $1 per year.

Partly that's because he has so much money from his shares that he does not need a few extra million dollars of salary. But perhaps you remember one other famous Silicon Valley entrepreneur who earned exactly the same $1.00 salary: Steve Jobs of Apple.

When Jobs came back to Apple in 1997,

Part 4 A giant of the Internet

he took a salary of just $1 a year. From 1997 until 2011, when he died, Jobs earned a total of $15.00. At the same time, Jobs was revolutionizing the music business, the phone business, and the publishing business, and building Apple into the most valuable company in the world.

When Steve Jobs died in 2012, Mark Zuckerberg published a short press release. "Steve," it said, "thank you for being a mentor and a friend. Thanks for showing that what you build can change the world. I will miss you."

In Silicon Valley, people with small salaries often accomplish the biggest things.

Mark Zuckerberg, like Steve Jobs before him, is a visionary who has changed the world. Still in his twenties, he is already one of the giants of the Internet age.

Word List

- 本文で使われている全ての語を掲載しています（LEVEL 1、2）。ただし、LEVEL 3以上は、中学校レベルの語を含みません。
- 語形が規則変化する語の見出しは原形で示しています。不規則変化語は本文中で使われている形になっています。
- 一般的な意味を紹介していますので、一部の語で本文で実際に使われている品詞や意味と合っていないことがあります。
- 品詞は以下のように示しています。

名 名詞	代 代名詞	形 形容詞	副 副詞	動 動詞	助動 助動詞
前 前置詞	接 接続詞	間 間投詞	冠 冠詞	略 略語	俗 俗語
頭 接頭語	尾 接尾語	記 記号	関 関係代名詞		

A

- **Aaron Sorkin** アーロン・ソーキン《アメリカの劇作家、脚本家。映画『ソーシャルネットワーク』の脚本を手がけた》
- **ability** 名 ①能力 ②才能
- **Academy Award** アカデミー賞《米国の映画賞》
- **Accel Partners** アクセルパートナーズ《投資会社》
- **accept** 動 受け入れる
- **access** 名（システムなどへの）アクセス
- **Accidental Billionaires: The Founding of Facebook** 『ジ・アクシデンタル・ビリオネア』《「思いがけず偶発的に億万長者になった人」、ベン・メズリック著、2009》
- **accomplish** 動 成し遂げる、果たす
- **account** 名 勘定、預金口座 動《– for ～》～（の割合）を占める
- **accurate** 名 正確な、間違いのない
- **accurately** 副 正確に、正しく、きちんと
- **accuse** 動《– of ～》～（の理由）で告訴［非難］する
- **active** 形 ①活動的な ②積極的な
- **activity** 名 活動、事業
- **actually** 副 実際に、本当に、実は
- **ad** 略 advertisement（広告、宣伝）の略
- **Adam D'Angelo** アダム・ダンジェロ《ザッカーバーグの高校時代からの友人、後にフェイスブックのCTO》
- **adapt** 動 適応する［させる］
- **add** 動 ①加える、足す ②言い添える、書き添える
- **addicted to**《be –》中毒の、病みつきの
- **address** 名 住所、アドレス
- **Adidas** 名 アディダス《スポーツ用品メーカー》
- **administrator** 名 経営者、理事、管理者
- **adult** 名 大人、成人
- **advance** 熟 in advance 前もって、あらかじめ
- **advertise** 動 広告する、宣伝する
- **advertisement** 名 広告、宣伝
- **advertiser** 名 広告主
- **advertising** 名 広告、宣伝 形 広

Word List

告の
- **advice** 名 忠告, 助言, 意見
- **afraid of** 《be –》～を恐れる, ～を怖がる
- **aged** 形 ～歳である
- **agency** 名 代理店, 仲介
- **all at once** 一度にそろって, 出し抜けに
- **allow** 動 ①許す ②与える
- **along with** ～と一緒に
- **although** 接 ～だけれども, とはいえ
- **Amazon** 名 アマゾン《オンライン通販サイト》
- **ambitious** 形 大望のある, 野心的な
- **America** 名 アメリカ《国名・大陸》
- **American** 形 アメリカ(人)の
- **Andover** 名 アンドーバー《フィリップス・エクセター高校の別称》
- **Andrew McCollum** アンドリュー・マッコラム《ハーバードの学生, フェイスブックのロゴマークを手がけた》
- **Android** 名 アンドロイド《Googleが開発した携帯端末用のオープンソースのOS》
- **Android mobile** アンドロイド携帯《アンドロイドのオペレーティングシステムを搭載したスマートフォン》
- **Anglo-Saxon** 形 アングロサクソン系の
- **anniversary** 名 記念日, 記念祭
- **announce** 動 (人に)知らせる, 公表する
- **annoy** 動 いらいらさせる
- **another** 熟 one another お互い
- **anti-FARC** 名 反コロンビア革命軍団体
- **anybody** 代 誰でも
- **anymore** 副 《通例否定文, 疑問文で》今はもう, これ以上
- **anyone** 代 ①《否定文で》誰も(～ない) ②《肯定文で》誰でも
- **anywhere** 副 どこででも
- **AOL** 名 エーオーエル《インターネットサービス会社》
- **API** 略 エーピーアイ《アプリケーション・プログラミング・インターフェース, application programming interfaceの略称》
- **apologize** 動 謝る, わびる
- **app** 略 アプリケーション・プログラム《application programの略》
- **appeal** 動 ①求める, 頼む ②(人心に)訴える
- **appealing** 形 心を動かすような, 魅力的な
- **appear** 動 ①(記事などが新聞に)出る ②出演する
- **Apple** 名 アップル社《アメリカのデジタル家電およびソフトウェアを設計製造する多国籍企業》
- **application** 名 ①申し込み, 申請 ②アプリケーション《略称app》
- **application programming interface** アプリケーション・プログラミング・インターフェース, エーピーアイ《略称API》
- **approach** 名 学習[研究]方法, 手引き
- **Ardsley High School** アーズレイ高校《ザッカーバーグが最初に通った地元の公立校》
- **argument** 名 議論, 論争
- **Arielle** 名 アリエル《ザッカーバーグの妹》
- **arrest** 動 逮捕する
- **arrogant** 形 尊大な, 傲慢な, 無礼な, 横柄な
- **article** 名 (新聞・雑誌などの)記事, 論文
- **artist** 名 芸術家

- **as** 熟 as well as ～と同様に times as … as A Aの～倍の…
- **Asana** 名 アーサナ《ダスティン・モスコヴィッツがフェイスブック退社後に起した会社》
- **ashram** 名 ヒンドゥー教の僧院
- **Association of Black Harvard Women** ハーバード黒人女性連盟
- **athletic** 形 強健な, 運動が得意な
- **attention** 名 注意, 注目 pay no attention 気に留めない, 目もくれない
- **attract** 動 引きつける, 魅了する
- **attractive** 形 魅力的な
- **auction company** 競売会社
- **audio** 形 オーディオの, 音声の
- **author** 名 著者, 作家
- **automate** 動 自動化する, オートメ化する
- **automatically** 副 無意識に, 自動的に
- **available** 形 利用[使用]できる
- **award** 名 賞

B

- **back** 熟 go back to ～に帰る[戻る], ～に遡る, (中断していた作業に)再び取り掛かる
- **background** 名 ①背景 ②経歴
- **backpacking** 名 バックパックを背負ってあちこちを見聞して回る旅 go backpacking バックパックを背負った周遊旅行に出る
- **bad-boy** 形 不良少年の, 素行の良くない
- **baggy** 形 だぶだぶの, たるんだ
- **ban** 動 禁止する
- **Barack Obama** バラク・オバマ《アメリカ合衆国第44代大統領, 1961-》
- **Barack Obama campaign** 大統領選のためにバラク・オバマ氏が行った選挙活動
- **base** 動《- on ～》～に基礎[本拠地]を置く, 基づく
- **basement** 名 地下(室)
- **basic** 形 基礎の, 基本的な
- **basically** 副 基本的には, 大筋では
- **bathroom** 名 手洗い, トイレ
- **Beacon** 名 ビーコン《ネット上で買い物をすると, 友人たちにその詳細が通知されるというフェイスブック上のサービス》
- **bed** 熟 get out of bed 起きる, 寝床を離れる
- **beer** 名 ビール
- **beginner** 名 初心者
- **beginning** 名 初め, 始まり
- **behave** 動 振る舞う
- **behavior** 名 振る舞い, 態度
- **behind** 前 ～の後ろに, ～の背後に
- **Beijing Olympics** 北京オリンピック《2008年開催》
- **belong** 動《- to ～》～に属する
- **below** 副 下の方に[へ]
- **Ben Mezrich** ベン・メズリック《映画『ソーシャルネットワーク』の元となったThe Accidental Billionaires: The Founding of Facebookの著者》
- **beyond** 前 ～を越えて, ～の向こうに
- **bill** 名 請求書, 勘定書
- **Bill Clinton** ビル・クリントン《アメリカ合衆国第42代大統領, 1946-》
- **Bill Gates** ビル・ゲイツ《マイクロソフト社の創業者, 1955-》
- **billion** 名 10億
- **billionaire** 名 億万長者
- **birth** 名 誕生
- **bitch** 名 あばずれ女

Word List

- **blog** 名 日記形式のウェブサイト, ブログ, web log の略から 動 ブログに書く
- **blond** 形 金髪の
- **board** 名 重役会
- **bold** 形 勇敢な, 大胆な, 力強い
- **Bono** 名 ボノ《アイルランドのロックバンド, U2 (ユーツー) のボーカル》
- **bonus** 名 ボーナス, 慰労金
- **boom** 名 ブーム, 急成長
- **booming** 形 成長著しい
- **boring** 形 うんざりさせる, 退屈な
- **Boston University** ボストン大学
- **boundary** 名 境界線, 限界
- **box office** (映画館・劇場の) チケット売り場
- **boyfriend** 名 男友だち
- **brand** 名 ブランド, 商標, 品種
- **Brazil** 名 ブラジル《国》
- **Brazilian** 名 ブラジル人
- **break into** ～に侵入する
- **Breyer, Jim** (ジム・) ブレイヤー《アクセル・パートナーズ社の重役》
- **brilliantly** 副 すばらしく, 際立って
- **Brown University** ブラウン大学
- **businesslike** 形 実際的な, 仕事のような
- **but** 熟 not ～ but … ～ではなくて…
- **by chance** 偶然に

C

- **California** 名 カリフォルニア《地名》
- **California Institute of Technology** カリフォルニア工科大学
- **Cameron Winkelvoss** キャメロン・ウィンクルヴォス《ザッカーバーグに対し, フェイスブックの創設について訴訟を起すウィンクルヴォス双子の一人》
- **campaign** 名 ①キャンペーン (活動, 運動) ②政治運動, 選挙運動
- **campus** 名 キャンパス, (大学などの) 構内
- **capital** 名 資本 (金) 形 資本の
- **captain** 名 長, 主将
- **care about** ～を気に掛ける
- **Caribbean** 形 カリブ海の
- **cash** 名 現金 (払い)
- **celebrate** 動 祝う, 祝福する
- **celebrity** 名 有名人, セレブ
- **centimeter** 名 センチメートル《長さの単位》
- **CEO** 略 最高経営責任者 (= Chief Executive Officer)
- **certain** 形 ①(人が) 確信した ②とある
- **certainly** 副 確かに, 必ず
- **challenger** 名 挑戦者, (投票が) 無効であると主張する人
- **champagne** 名 シャンパン
- **chance** 熟 by chance 偶然, たまたま
- **channel** 名 (テレビの) チャンネル, 局
- **chant** 名 詠唱
- **charge** 名 責任 in charge of ～を任されて, ～を担当して, ～の責任を負って
- **Charlie Cheever** チャーリー・チーバー《フェイスブック幹部, フェイスブックコネクトを開発した》
- **Chase Manhattan Bank** チェース・マンハッタン銀行
- **chat** 名 チャット《インターネットを用いたリアルタイムなコミュニケ

ーションサービス》
- **cheat** 動だます, ごまかす
- **cheerleader** 名チアリーダー
- **chief** 名頭, 長 形最高位の, 第一の, 主要な
- **chief technical officer** 最高技術責任者《略称, CTO》
- **childhood** 名幼年[子ども]時代
- **China** 名中国《国名》
- **Chinese** 形中国(人)の
- **Choe, David** (デイビッド・)チョー《グラフィティアーティスト, 壁などにスプレーなどで描かれる落書きで, 前衛的芸術》
- **chorus** 名合唱(団)
- **Chris DeWolfe** クリス・デウォルフ《企業家, MySpaceのCEO》
- **Chris Hughes** クリス・ヒューズ《ザッカーバーグの元ルームメイト, フェイスブック創設者の一人であり, スポークスマンを務めた》
- **Christmas** 名クリスマス
- **Christopher Ma** クリストファー・マ《ワシントンポストのメディア開発部門に勤める》
- **CityVille** 名シティビル《フェイスブック上に公開された街作りゲーム》
- **Clarium Capital** クラリウム・キャピタル《ピーター・シールが立ち上げた投資基金》
- **Claude** 名クロード, 男子の名前
- **clear** 形はっきりした, 明白な
- **clever** 形巧妙な
- **click** 動(ボタンを)カチッと押す, クリックする
- **climb into** 〜に乗り込む
- **co-founded** 形共同設立の
- **co-founder** 名共同設立者
- **coach** 名コーチ, 指導者
- **cocaine** 名コカイン, 麻薬の一種
- **code** 動プログラムする 名記号,

符号
- **colleague** 名同僚, 仲間
- **Colombia** 名コロンビア(共和国)
- **colorblind** 色覚異常の, 色弱の
- **colorful** 形①カラフルな, 派手な ②生き生きとした
- **Columbia (University)** 名コロンビア大学
- **combine** 動合併させる
- **come out** 出てくる, 姿を現す, 世に出る
- **coming** 名到来, 来ること
- **comment** 名論評, コメント 動論評する, コメントする
- **communicate** 動①連絡する ②理解し合う
- **communication** 名伝えること, 情報伝達
- **compare** 動比較する, 対照する
- **competition** 名競争, 競合
- **complain** 動①不平[苦情]を言う[訴える], ぶつぶつ言う
- **complete** 形完全な, 完成した 動完成させる
- **completely** 副完全に, すっかり
- **compressed** 形圧縮された
- **concentrate** 動集中する
- **concept** 名テーマ, (計画案などの)基本的な方向
- **confirm** 動確かめる, 確かにする
- **connect** 動つながる, つなぐ, 関係づける
- **connected** 形結合した, 関係のある
- **Connecticut** 名コネティカット州《地名》
- **connection** 名つながり, 関係
- **ConnectU** 名コネクトユー《ウィンクルヴォス双子が発表したソーシャルネットワーキングサービス》
- **conservative** 形保守的な

Word List

- **consume** 動摂取する, 消費する
- **consumption** 名消費
- **continuous** 形継続する, 絶え間ない
- **contract** 名契約(書), 協定
- **control** 動①管理[支配]する ②抑制する, コントロールする
- **conversation** 名会話, 会談
- **coordinate** 動(各部が)調和して働く[機能する], 調和させる
- **copy** 動まねる, コピーする
- **copyright** 名著作権, 版権
- **core** 名核心, 中心, 芯 core value 基本理念
- **Cornell University** コーネル大学
- **corporate** 形企業の corporate culture 企業風土, 社風 corporate headquarter 本社
- **corporation** 名法人, (株式)会社
- **cost** 名値段, 費用 動(金・費用が)かかる, (～を)要する
- **could** 熟 How could ～? 何だって～なんてことがありえようか?
- **counselor** 名カウンセラー, 相談役
- **counterattack** 名反撃
- **Course Match** コースマッチ《ザッカーバーグが2003年, ハーバード在学中に作った, 同じクラスを履修している他の学生のリストを参照できるようにするプログラム》
- **court** 名法廷, 裁判所
- **cover** 動①覆う, 包む be covered with ～で覆われている
- **cow** 名雌牛, 乳牛
- **crash** 名暴落, 恐慌, 破綻 動クラッシュする, 故障する
- **crazy** 形狂気の, ばかげた, 頭のおかしい
- **cream** 名クリーム

- **create** 動創造する, 生み出す, 引き起こす
- **creative** 形創造力のある, 独創的な
- **creator** 名創作者, 創造者
- **credit card** クレジット・カード
- **crimson** 形①深紅色 ②ハーバード大学《俗》
- **critic** 名批評家, 評論家
- **crowd** 名群集, 聴衆
- **crowd sourcing** クラウドソーシング《不特定多数の人々に無償または低額報酬で(インターネットを介して)仕事を依頼すること》
- **CTO** 略最高技術責任者《chief technical officerの略》
- **cultivate** 動(才能などを)養う, 育成する
- **cultural** 形文化的な
- **curly** 形巻き毛の
- **Cyworld** 名サイワールド《韓国で主流のソーシャルネットワーキングサービス》

D

- **D'Angelo, Adam** (アダム・)ダンジェロ《ザッカーバーグの高校時代からの友人, フェイスブックのCTOを務めた》
- **Da Vinci Code**『ダ・ヴィンチ・コード』《ダン・ブラウン著の大ベストセラー長編推理小説》
- **damage** 動損害を与える, 傷つける
- **Dan Brown** ダン・ブラウン《『ダ・ヴィンチ・コード』の著者, 1964–》
- **Dartmouth University** ダートマス大学
- **data** 名データ, 情報
- **database** 名データベース, 系統的に管理された情報の集まり, またそ

れらを管理するシステム
- **dating** 名デート
- **David Choe** デイビッド・チョー《グラフィティアーティスト, 1976–》
- **David Fincher** デヴィッド・フィンチャー《映画監督, 映画『ソーシャルネットワーク』の監督, 1962–》
- **David Newman** デヴィッド・ニューマン《幼少期のザッカーバーグのプログラミングの家庭教師》
- **deal** 名取引 make a deal 取引する
- **debate** 動討論する
- **debut** 名デビュー, 初登場 動デビューする
- **decision** 名決定, 決心
- **decorate** 動飾る
- **demand** 名要求, 需要
- **Democratic** 形民主党の
- **dentist** 名歯医者
- **department** 名課, 局
- **describe** 動(言葉で)描写する, 特色を述べる, 説明する
- **description** 名(言葉で)記述(すること), 描写(すること)
- **deserve** 動(〜を)受けるに足る[当然である]
- **design** 動設計する 名デザイン, 設計(図)
- **despite** 前〜にもかかわらず
- **detail** 名《-s》詳細
- **developer** 名開発者
- **development** 名①発達, 発展 ②開発
- **difficulty** 名①難局 ②《-ties》財政困難
- **digital** 形数字の, 数字表示の, デジタルの
- **direction** 名方向, 方角
- **director** 名管理者, 指導者, 監督
- **directory** 名住所氏名録

- **disappointed** 形がっかりした, 失望した
- **disaster** 名災難, まったくの失敗
- **discipline** 名鍛錬, 学問(の分野)
- **discount** 名ディスカウント, 割引
- **discuss** 動議論[検討]する
- **discussion** 名討議, 討論
- **dishonest** 形不誠実な
- **disloyal** 形不義の
- **Divya Narendra** ディヴィヤ・ナレンドラ《ザッカーバーグに対しフェイスブックの創設に関して訴訟を起こした一人》
- **Dobbs Ferry** ドブズ・フェリー《ニューヨーク郊外の町, ザッカーバーグの出身地》
- **document** 名文書, 記録
- **domain** 名(インターネットの)ドメイン《インターネット上の住所のようなもの》domain name ドメイン名, ドメイン・ネーム
- **dominance** 名支配, 優勢
- **Don Graham** ドン・グラハム《ワシントンポストの最高経営責任者》
- **Donna** 名ダナ《ザッカーバーグの妹》
- **dormitory** 名寄宿舎, 寮
- **dotcom** 名ドットコム企業, インターネット関連企業
- **dotcom crash** 名ITバブルの崩壊
- **double** 動 double trouble 非常に面倒なこと 動2倍になる
- **drama** 名劇, ドラマ
- **dramatic** 形劇的な
- **drawing** 名絵を描くこと
- **Dreamweaver** 名ドリームウィーバー《マクロメディアが開発したウェブサイト作成ソフト》
- **dressing** 名衣装, 装い
- **drinking** 名飲酒 drinking game

Word List

(酒の)飲み比べ **drinking age** 飲酒年齢
- **drive away** 車で走り去る
- **drop out** 退学する, 中退する
- **drove** 動 drive (車で行く)の過去
- **drunken** 形 酔っ払った
- **Dustin Moskovitz** ダスティン・モスコヴィッツ《ザッカーバーグの元ルームメイト, フェイスブック創設者の一人, 1984–》

E

- **e-mail** 名 電子メール 動 電子メールを[で]送る
- **earn** 動 儲ける, 稼ぐ
- **easily** 副 容易に, たやすく, 苦もなく
- **eBay** 名 イーベイ《オンラインオークションサイト》
- **economics** 名 経済学
- **economy** 名 経済, 財政
- **Eduardo Saverin** エドゥアルド・サベリン《ブラジル人, ハーバード時代にザッカーバーグの共同出資者になる》
- **education** 名 教育, 教養
- **Edward** エドワード《ザッカーバーグの父, ニューヨーク郊外の自宅で歯科医院を営む》
- **effect** 名 影響, 効果
- **Efrusy, Kevin** (ケヴィン・)エフラシー《アクセルパートナーズに所属する投資家》
- **Egypt** 名 エジプト《国名》
- **election** 名 選挙
- **electricity** 名 電気
- **elite** 形 エリートの, 一流の, えり抜きの
- **Elliot** エリオット《ザッカーバーグのミドルネーム》
- **elsewhere** 副 どこかほかの所で
- **embarrassed** 形 恥ずかしい, きまりの悪い思いをして
- **Empath** 名 エンパス《クリス・ヒューズの愛称, 周囲の人たちの感情を鋭敏に感じ取ることができる特殊能力者の意》
- **employee** 名 従業員
- **enable** 動 (〜することを)可能にする, 容易にする
- **encourage** 動 ①勇気づける ②促進する
- **end up** 結局[最後は]〜になる
- **end-of-semester** 名 学期末
- **enemy** 名 敵
- **engagement ads** エンゲージメントアド《ソーシャル型広告。利用者がコメントをつけたり, バーチャルギフトを贈ったり, 広告内で直接ブランドの用意するフェイスブックページのファンになったりできる》
- **enormous** 形 非常に大きい, 巨大な
- **entertaining** 形 愉快な, 面白い
- **entrepreneur** 名 企業家, 事業家
- **entrepreneurial** 形 企業家の, 事業家の
- **environment** 名 環境
- **epic poem** 叙事詩
- **equally** 副 等しく, 平等に
- **Esquire** エスクァイア《アメリカの男性誌》
- **establish** 動 確立する, 設置[設立]する
- **etc** 略 〜など, その他 (= et cetera)
- **eventually** 副 結局は, ついには
- **ever-changing** 形 絶えず変化する
- **everybody** 代 誰でも, 皆
- **everyone** 代 誰でも, 皆
- **everything** 代 すべてのこと[も

THE MARK ZUCKERBERG STORY

の], 何でも, 何もかも
- **evolve** 動 進化する, 発展する
- **exam** 名《略式》テスト, 試験
- **except** 前 ～を除いて, ～のほかは
- **exception** 名 例外
- **exchanging** 名 交換
- **executive** 形 管理や経営などを行う 名 重役, 役員, 幹部
- **exist** 動 存在する
- **exit** 動 退場する, 去る
- **expand** 動 ①広げる, 拡張[拡大]する ②発展させる, 拡充する
- **expansion** 名 拡大, 拡張
- **expect** 動 予期[予測]する, (当然のこととして)期待する
- **experienced** 形 経験豊富な
- **experiment** 名 実験, 試み
- **express** 動 表現する, 述べる
- **expression** 名 表現, 言い回し
- **expressionless** 形 感情をこめない
- **extra** 形 余分の
- **extraordinarily** 副 異常に, 並外れて
- **extremely** 副 非常に, 極度に

F

- **face-to-face** 副 面と向かって, 直接に
- **facebook** 名 大学が発行する新入生名簿
- **Facebook** 名 フェイスブック《ザッカーバーグが2004年に発表したソーシャルネットワーキングサービス, 当初はハーバード大学生の交流のためのサービスであったが, 現在では一般向けとなっている》
- **Facebook Connect** フェイスブック・コネクト《フェイスブックが持つ情報を外部サイトで利用できる機能》
- **Facemash** 名 フェイスマッシュ《ザッカーバーグが学生時代に発表した, ハーバード大学生の容姿格付けを行わせるウェブサイト》
- **fail** 動 失敗する
- **failure** 名 失敗
- **fairer** 形 より公正な, より良い
- **fall semester** 秋学期
- **fantasy** 名 空想, 幻想
- **FARC** 略 コロンビア革命軍《中南米最大の反政府武装組織, Fuerzas Armadas Revolucionarias de Colombiaの略》
- **FarmVille** 名 ファームヴィル《農場を経営するゲーム》
- **fast-changing** 形 急速に変化する
- **fast-growing** 形 急成長の
- **FBI** 略 連邦捜査局《Federal Bureau of Investigationの略》
- **feature** 名 ①特色, 特徴, 造作 ②機構
- **feed** 名 供給 News Feed ニュースフィード《新着情報や更新情報などをある決まった形式で配信する仕組みや, それを通じて配信されるニュースのこと》
- **fencing** 名 フェンシング
- **fiction** 名 フィクション, 作り話
- **fight back** 反撃する
- **Fight Club** 『ファイト・クラブ』《映画, 1999》
- **file-sharing** 形 ファイル共有の
- **final** 形 最後の, 最終の
- **finished** 形 終わった, 仕上がった
- **firm** 名 会社, 事務所
- **firmly** 副 堅く, 確固として
- **firstly** 副 初めに, まず第一に
- **fix** 動 修理する

Word List

- **Flash** 名 フラッシュ《マクロメディアが開発したアニメ、ゲーム、ウェブサイトなどを作成するためのソフトウェア》
- **flat** 形 平らな、平坦な
- **flavor** 名 風味、味
- **fleece** 名 フリース素材、フリース素材の服
- **flexible** 形 (考えなどが)柔軟性のある、順応性のある
- **Flickr** 名 フリッカー《写真の共有を目的とした画像投稿コミュニティーサイト》
- **float** 動 ①浮く、浮かぶ ②漂流する
- **Florida** 名 フロリダ《地名》
- **focus** 名 ①焦点、ピント ②関心の的、着眼点 動 ①焦点を合わせる ②(関心・注意を)集中させる
- **foothold** 名 足がかり、地盤
- **foreword** 名 序文
- **format** 名 形式、型
- **former** 形 前の、先の、以前の
- **FOSS** 略 シェリル・サンドバーグの友達の意《friend of Sheryl Sandbergの略》
- **found** 動 設立する、創立する
- **founder** 名 創立者、設立者
- **framework** 名 骨組み、構造、組織
- **France** 名 フランス《国名》
- **Franklin Pierce** フランクリン・ピアース《第14代アメリカ合衆国大統領、1804-1869》
- **fraternity** 名 社交クラブ
- **freckle** 名 そばかす
- **freeze** 動 (銀行の預金や資産を)凍結する
- **French** 形 フランス(人・語)の 名 フランス語
- **Friendster** 名 フレンドスター《ソーシャルネットワーキングサービスの草分け的存在》
- **Frisson** 名 フリッソン《ピーター・シールがサンフランシスコに所有するナイトクラブ》
- **front line** 名 最前線、第一線 形 最前線の、第一線の
- **froze** 動 freeze (凍る)の過去
- **fuck up** 台無しにする、しくじる
- **fulfill** 動 (要求・条件を)満たす
- **fund** 名 資金、基金、財源
- **futures market** 先物市場

G

- **GAFA** 略 Google, Apple, Facebook, Amazonの四つのインターネット企業の頭文字を取った略称
- **gang** 名 ギャング、非行少年グループ
- **gas** 名 ガソリン
- **generate** 動 生み出す、引き起こす
- **German** 名 ドイツ語
- **Germany** 名 ドイツ《国名》
- **get** 熟 get in 加入する、入会する、入学する get into trouble 面倒を起こす get one's revenge 恨みを晴らす get out of bed 起きる、寝床を離れる get ready 用意[支度]をする get someone to do (人)に〜させる[してもらう] get started 始める get 〜 to 〜に…するよう説得する
- **giant** 名 巨匠 形 巨大な、偉大な
- **gifted** 形 才能のある、知能のある
- **girlfriend** 名 女友だち
- **global** 形 地球規模の、世界的な、国際的な
- **go** 熟 go back to 〜に帰る[戻る]、〜に遡る、(中断していた作業に)再び取り掛かる go backpacking バックパックを背負った周遊旅行に出る go down 少なくなる go on 続く、続ける、進み続ける、起こる、発生する go

- **on to** 〜に移る、〜に取り掛かる **go public** (企業が)株式を公開する **go with** 〜と一緒に行く、〜と調和する、〜にとても似合う
- **Goldman Sachs** ゴールドマンサックス《世界最大級の投資銀行、1869–》
- **good-looking** 形 顔立ちのよい、ハンサムな、きれいな
- **Google** 名 グーグル《検索エンジンGoogleを運営するソフトウェア会社、1998–》
- **Google Android** グーグル・アンドロイド《Googleが開発した携帯端末用のオープンソースのOS》
- **governed** 形 統制された
- **government** 名 政府
- **graduate** 名 卒業生、(〜学校の)出身者
- **graduate student** 大学院生
- **graduation** 名 卒業(式)
- **graffiti** 名 graffito(落書き)の複数形
- **Graham, Don** (ドン・)グラハム《ワシントンポストの最高経営責任者》
- **graph** 名 グラフ、図表
- **Greek** 名 ギリシャ語
- **Group** 名 グループ《フェイスブック内で投稿した書き込みや写真を登録したグループの中でのみ共有することができる機能》
- **grow up** 成長する、大人になる
- **growing** 形 成長期にある、大きくなりつつある
- **grown-up** 形 成長した
- **guaranteed** 形 請け負っている、約束されている
- **guess** 動 推測する
- **guest** 名 客、ゲスト
- **gun** 名 銃
- **Gwen Stefani** グウェン・ステファニー《女性歌手、1969–》

H

- **hackathon** 名 ハッカーソン《開発者たちが集まり、協議・協力しながら集中的にプログラム開発を行う場》
- **hacker** 名 ①プログラム開発を行う人 ②コンピュータ・システムに不法に侵入し、データの窃盗や改ざんを行う人
- **Hacker Way** ハッカーウェイ(ハッカーの流儀)
- **hacking** 名 ①コンピュータ・プログラミング ②コンピュータ・システムへの不法侵入行為
- **handle** 動 操縦する、取り扱う
- **hands-on** 形 実地の、実践の
- **handsome** 形 顔立ちの良い、(男性が)ハンサムな
- **hardly** 副 ほとんど〜でない
- **hardware** 名 (コンピュータの)ハードウェア
- **Harkness table method** ハークネス・メソッド《教師と少数の生徒が円卓に座り、ディスカッション形式で行われる授業方法》
- **Harry Lewis** ハリー・ルイス《ハーバード大学の人気教師》
- **Harvard Crimson** ハーバード・クリムゾン《ハーバード大学の学生新聞》
- **Harvard Investment Club** ハーバード・インベストメント・クラブ《ハーバード大学の投資クラブ(少人数で小口の資金を出し合い、投資の経験を積もうとするサークル)》
- **Harvard University** ハーバード大学《アメリカ最古の大学、1636–》
- **HarvardConnection** 名 ハーバードコネクション《ウィンクルヴォス双子とナレンドラ氏と共同で開発するはずであったソーシャルネットワ

Word List

- [ ] **hate** 動 嫌う, 憎む
- [ ] **help** 熟 help ~ with … …を〜の面で手伝う
- [ ] **hey** 間《呼びかけ・注意を促して》おい, ちょっと
- [ ] **high-school** 名 高校
- [ ] **hire** 動 雇う
- [ ] **Hispanic** 形 ラテンアメリカ系の
- [ ] **historic** 形 歴史的な
- [ ] **hobby** 名 趣味, 得意なこと
- [ ] **Hoffman, Reid** (リード・) ホフマン《リンクドイン社の創立者》
- [ ] **Hollywood** 名 ハリウッド《地名》
- [ ] **Homer** 名 ホメロス《古代ギリシャの詩人》
- [ ] **Hosni Mubarak** ホスニー・ムバラク《共和制エジプト第4代大統領, 1928–》
- [ ] **host** 動《インターネット上での情報の表示場所を》間貸しする
- [ ] **How could ~?** 何だって〜なんてことがありえようか?
- [ ] **Howard Winkelvoss** ハワード・ウィンクルヴォス《ザッカーバーグに対して訴訟を起こしたウィンクルヴォス双子の父, 企業家》
- [ ] **however** 接 けれども, だが
- [ ] **huge** 形 巨大な, ばく大な
- [ ] **hugely** 副 非常に, 大いに
- [ ] **Hughes, Chris** (クリス・) ヒューズ《ザッカーバーグの元ルームメイト, フェイスブック創設者の一人でありスポークスマンを務めた》

I

- [ ] **I wish that nobody had ~.** だれも〜しないでくれたらよかったのに。《仮定法》
- [ ] **identical** 形 まったく同じ
- [ ] **identical twins** 一卵性双生児
- [ ] **identity** 名 人格
- [ ] **Illinois Senator** イリノイ州上院議員
- [ ] **image** 名 印象, イメージ
- [ ] **immediately** 副 すぐに, 直ちに
- [ ] **immigrant** 名 移民, 移住者
- [ ] **impact** 名 影響力, 効果
- [ ] **implement** 動 道具[手段]を提供する
- [ ] **implementation** 名 実行, 履行
- [ ] **impressed** 形 感動して, 感銘を受けて
- [ ] **impression** 名 印象, 感想
- [ ] **improve** 動 改善する[させる], 進歩する
- [ ] **improvement** 名 改良, 改善
- [ ] **inch** 名 インチ《長さの単位, 1インチ = 2.54センチ》
- [ ] **include** 動 含む, 勘定に入れる
- [ ] **included** 形 含まれた
- [ ] **including** 前 〜を含めて, 込みで
- [ ] **income** 名 収入, 所得, 収益
- [ ] **increase** 動 増加[増強]する, 増やす, 増える
- [ ] **indeed** 副 実際, 本当に
- [ ] **independent** 形 独立した, 独自の
- [ ] **India** 名 インド《国名》
- [ ] **Indian** 形 インド(人)の
- [ ] **industry** 名 産業, 工業
- [ ] **influence** 動 影響をおよぼす
- [ ] **input** 動 入力する
- [ ] **inspired** 形 触発された, 心を動かされた
- [ ] **Instagram** 名 インスタグラム《スマートフォンアプリ, 写真に特化したソーシャルネットワーキングサービス》
- [ ] **instant** 形 即時の, 即席の

- **instant messaging** インスタント・メッセージ《インターネットに接続している特定ユーザーを呼び出しパソコン上でチャットやファイル転送を可能にする機能》
- **instead** 副 その代わりに instead of ～の代わりに, ～をしないで
- **institute** 名 協会, 研究所
- **institution** 名 学会
- **interact** 動 ～と影響しあう, ～と相互に作用する
- **interested** 形 興味を持った, 関心のある
- **interesting** 形 おもしろい, 興味を起こさせる
- **interestingly** 副 面白いことに, 興味深いことに
- **interface** 名 インターフェース, 情報の仲介をするもの application programming interface アプリケーション・プログラミング・インターフェース, エーピーアイ《略称API》
- **Interpublic** 名 インターパブリック《世界最大級の広告代理会社》
- **intoxicated** 形 (酒に)酔って
- **invent** 動 発明[考案]する
- **invention** 名 発明(品)
- **invest** 動 投資する, (金・精力など)を注ぐ
- **investing** 名 投資
- **investment** 名 投資, 出資
- **investment bank** (証券)投資銀行
- **investment club** 投資クラブ《少人数で小口の資金を出し合い, 投資の経験を積もうとするサークル》
- **investor** 名 出資者, 投資家
- **invitation** 名 招待(状)
- **involve** 動 含む, 伴う
- **involved** 形 巻き込まれている, 関連する
- **iOS** 名 アイオーエス《アップル社が開発・提供するオペレーティングシステム》
- **iPhone** 名 アイフォン《アップル社から発売されたスマートフォン》
- **IQ** 名 知能指数《intelligence quotient の略》
- **Iran** 名 イラン《国名》
- **ironic** 形 皮肉な
- **issue** 名 ①問題, 論点 ②発行物
- **It is ～ for someone to …** (人)が…するのは～だ
- **itself** 代 それ自体, それ自身
- **Ivy League** アイビーリーグ《米国北部の名門大学の総称》

J

- **jacket** 名 短い上着
- **Jaws** 名『ジョーズ』《巨大人食いザメの恐怖を描いたホラー小説, スティーブン・スピルバーグ監督で映画化された. 1975》
- **jeans** 名 ジーンズ, ジーパン
- **Jewish** 形 ユダヤ人の, ユダヤ教の
- **Jim Breyer** ジム・ブレイヤー《アクセル社の重役社員》
- **Jobs, Steve** (スティーブ・)ジョブズ《アップル社の共同設立者の一人, 1955-2011》
- **John** 名 ジョン《男子の名前》
- **journalist** 名 報道関係者, ジャーナリスト
- **just** 熟 just as のときと同じように just then そのとたんに

K

- **Karen** カレン《ザッカーバーグの母, 元精神科医》
- **keen** 形 熱心な be keen to ～したがる

Word List

- **keep** 熟 keep in touch with ~と連絡を保つ keep on ~[-ing] ~し続ける, 繰り返し~する
- **Kevin Efrusy** ケヴィン・エフラシー《アクセルパートナーズに所属する投資家》
- **Kirkland House** カークランド・ハウス《ハーバード大学の学生寮の一つ》
- **kitesurf** 動 カイトサーフ(凧を用いたサーフィン)をする
- **Korea** 名 韓国《国名》

L

- **Latin** 名 ラテン語
- **launch** 動 (新製品などを)発表する, (事業などを)始める
- **Lawrence Summers** ローレンス・サマーズ《ザッカーバーグ在学中のハーバード大学学長, クリントン政権で財務長官を務めた, 1954-》
- **lawyer** 名 弁護士, 法律家
- **lead singer** (バンドの)リードボーカル
- **lead to** ~に至る, ~に通じる, ~を引き起こす
- **leadership** 名 指揮, リーダーシップ
- **league** 名 同盟, 連盟 Ivy League アイビーリーグ《米国北東部の名門大学の総称》
- **lecture** 名 講義
- **led** 動 lead (導く)の過去, 過去分詞
- **legal** 形 法律(上)の
- **legend** 名 伝説, 伝説的人物
- **less** 形 ~より小さい[少ない] 副 ~より少なく, ~ほどでなく much less まして~でない
- **lie** 動 うそをつく
- **lifestyle** 名 生活様式, ライフスタイル

- **limited liability company** LLC法人, 有限責任会社
- **linked** 形 関係した
- **LinkedIn** 名 リンクトイン《ビジネス関連に特化したソーシャルネットワーキングサービス》
- **list** 名 名簿, 一覧表 動 名簿[目録]に記入する
- **literature** 名 文学, 文芸
- **LLC** 略 有限責任会社《limited liability company の略》
- **lobby** 動 陳情する, ロビー活動をする
- **lockdown** 名 封鎖
- **log** 動 記録する log in ログインする, 所定の手続きを経てサービスの利用を開始する
- **logo** 名 ロゴ, 意匠文字
- **lonely** 形 孤独な, 心さびしい
- **long-term** 形 長期の
- **longer** 熟 no longer もはや~でない[~しない]
- **look for** ~を探す
- **Los Angeles** ロサンゼルス《米国の都市》
- **loyalty** 名 忠義, 忠誠
- **lying** 動 lie (うそをつく)の現在分詞

M

- **Macromedia** 名 マクロメディア《ソフトウェア会社, 2005年にアドビシステムズに買収される》
- **main** 形 主な, 主要な
- **mainly** 副 主に
- **major** 名 専攻科目 動 専攻する major in ~を専攻する
- **majority** 名 大多数, 大部分
- **make** 熟 make into ~を…に仕立てる make it possible for ~ to …

THE MARK ZUCKERBERG STORY

- ～が…できるようにする **make sure** 確かめる, 確認する
- **manage** 動 扱う, 経営[管理]する
- **management** 名 ①経営 ②運営, 管理(側)
- **manager** 名 経営者, 支配人, マネージャー
- **map** 動 地図をつくる, ～をはっきり描く
- **Mark Elliot Zuckerberg** マーク・エリオット・ザッカーバーグ《フェイスブック創立者, 1984-》
- **marketing** 形 マーケティングの, 市場調査・販売の **marketing director** マーケティング部長
- **mash** 動 すりつぶす, 押しつぶす 名 つぶされてドロドロになったもの
- **mass media** マスメディア, 新聞・雑誌・放送など
- **massacre** 名 大虐殺, 皆殺し
- **master** 名 管理人, 匠
- **Mastercard** 名 マスターカード《国際ブランドのクレジットカード, マスターカード社》
- **match** 名 ①試合, 勝負 ②相手, 釣り合うもの
- **maximize** 動 ～を最大限度にする
- **maximizing** 形 最大化する
- **meaning** 名 意味, 趣旨
- **meanwhile** 副 一方では
- **media** 名 メディア, マスコミ, 伝達・通信などの手段
- **meeting** 名 集まり, ミーティング, 面会
- **membership** 名 会員
- **Menlo Park** メンロパーク《地名》
- **mention** 動 (～について)述べる, 言及する
- **mentor** 名 師, 指導者
- **meritocratic** 形 実力主義的な
- **mess up** 台無しにする
- **messaging** 形 メッセージの **instant messageing** インスタント・メッセージ《インターネットに接続している特定ユーザーを呼び出しパソコン上でチャットやファイル転送を可能にする機能》
- **messenger** 名 (伝言・小包などの)配達人, 伝達者
- **method** 名 方法, 手段
- **Mezrich, Ben** (ベン・)メズリック《映画『ソーシャルネットワーク』の元となったThe Accidental Billionaires: The Founding of Facebookの著者》
- **Miami** 名 マイアミ《地名》
- **micro-blog** 名 ミニブログ《リアルタイムなコミュニケーションを提供するウェブ上のサービス》
- **Microsoft** 名 マイクロソフト《ビル・ゲイツとポール・アレンによって設立された世界最大級のコンピュータ・ソフトフェア会社》
- **Microsoft Windows** マイクロソフト・ウィンドウズ《マイクロソフト社が発売しているオペレーティングシステムのシリーズ》
- **mid-** 中間の, 中央の, 中頃などの意 **mid-2008** 2008年中頃
- **middle** 名 中間, 最中 **in the middle of** ～の真ん中[中ほど]に
- **might** 助 《mayの過去》～かもしれない
- **mind** 名 心, 記憶, 考え **take mind off** ～を忘れる, ～を意識から取り除く
- **minimum** 名 最低(限), 最小(限)
- **Mir Hossein Mousavi** ミール・ホセイン・ムーサヴィー《イラン・イスラム共和国第5代首相, 1941-》
- **mission** 名 使命, 任務
- **MIT** 略 マサチューセッツ工科大学《Massachusetts Institute of Technologyの略》
- **mix up** よく混ぜる, ごちゃ混ぜに

Word List

- する
- **Mixi** 名 ミクシィ《日本国内最大のソーシャルネットワーキングサービス》
- **mobile** 形 携帯できる 名 携帯電話
- **moment** 名 (特定の)時, 時期
- **monetize** 動 〜を収益化する
- **more** 熟 more and more ますます more than 〜以上
- **Moskovitz, Dustin** (ダスティン・)モスコヴィッツ《ザッカーバーグの元ルームメイト, フェイスブック創設者の一人, 1984–》
- **mostly** 副 主として, ほとんど
- **move out** 引っ越す, 立ち退く
- **movement** 名 (社会的な)運動
- **MTV** 名 ミュージックテレビジョン《アメリカの音楽番組専門のケーブルテレビ, Music Television の略》
- **much less** まして〜でない
- **musician** 名 音楽家
- **MySpace** 名 マイスペース《音楽・エンターテイメントに特化したソーシャルネットワーキングサービス》

N

- **Napster** 名 ナップスター《音楽ファイルを中心としたファイル共有ソフト》
- **name tag** 名札, ネームタグ
- **national** 形 国内規模の
- **nearby** 形 近くの, 間近の
- **nearly** 副 ほとんど
- **necessary** 形 必要な
- **negative** 形 否定的な, マイナスイメージの
- **Netflix** 名 ネットフリックス《オンライン DVD レンタル会社》
- **network** 名 回路, 網状組織, ネットワーキング
- **network effect** ネットワーク効果《ある財・サービスの利用者が増加すると, その財・サービスの利便性や効用が増加すること》
- **networking** 連絡網の作成, 人脈形成 **social networking** ソーシャルネットワーキング《特にインターネットを利用して, 友人・知人の輪を広げていくこと》形 連絡網の, 人脈作りの
- **New Jersey** ニュージャージー《地名》
- **New York** ニューヨーク《米国の都市;州》
- **New Yorker, The** ニューヨーカー《アメリカの総合週刊誌》
- **Newark** 名 ニューアーク《地名》
- **Newman, David** (デヴィッド・)ニューマン《幼少期のザッカーバーグのプログラミングの家庭教師》
- **news** 報道, ニュース, 知らせ
- **News Corporation** ニューズ・コーポレーション《大手新聞, テレビ, 映画会社などを傘下におさめる世界的なメディア・コングロマリット》
- **News Feed** ニュースフィード《新着情報や更新情報などをある決まった形式で配信する仕組みや, それを通じて配信されるニュースのこと》
- **NewsFeed** 名 ニュースフィード《フェイスブック上で何か行ったとき, 友人たちのページにその情報が通知されるシステム》
- **newspaper** 名 新聞(紙)
- **next big thing** 次なる目玉
- **niche** 形 特定の, 特定の人を狙った
- **nickname** 動 あだ名をつける, あだ名で呼ぶ
- **nightclub** 名 ナイトクラブ
- **nightlife** 名 バーやナイトクラブでの夜の遊び
- **Nike** 名 ナイキ《スポーツ関連商品を扱う世界的企業, 1968–》

- **no longer** もはや~しない
- **nobody** 代誰も[1人も]~ない
- **noise** 名騒音, 物音
- **nomination** 名指名, 任命, 推薦
- **none** 代(~の)誰も…ない
- **North America** 北米
- **North Carolina** ノースカロライナ《地名》
- **notable** 形注目に値する, 著名な
- **note** 名メモ, 覚え書き
- **now** 熟 right now 今すぐに, たった今
- **nowhere** 副どこにも~ない
- **nut** 名木の実, ナッツ

O

- **obviously** 副明らかに
- **offer** 動申し出る, 申し込む, 提供する 名提案, 提供
- **officer** 名幹部
- **officially** 副正式に
- **Oklahoma** 名オクラホマ《地名》
- **once** 熟 once every hundred years 100年に1回 at once すぐに, 同時に once a week 週に一回
- **online** 名オンライン 形オンラインの, ネットワーク上の
- **onto** 前~の上へ[に]
- **open registration** オープン登録制
- **open source software** オープン・ソース・ソフトウエア《ソースプログラムが公開されているソフトウエア》
- **open up** (商売などを)始める
- **opportunity** 名好機
- **Oprah Winfrey show** オプラ・ウィンフリー・ショー《オプラ・ウィンフリーが司会を務める, アメリカの人気トーク番組》
- **Oracle** 名オラクル・コーポレーション《世界最大級のコンピュータ・ソフト会社》
- **ordinary** 形 ①普通の ②並の, 平凡な
- **organize** 動組織する
- **organized** 形組織化された, よくまとまった
- **original** 形始めの, 本来の
- **originally** 副元は, 元来
- **Orkut** 名オルカット《グーグルが運営するソーシャルネットワーキングサービス》
- **Orkut Buyukkoten** オルカット・ブユコッテン《スタンフォードのユダヤ人学生, グーグルに入社しソーシャルネットワーキングサービス, オルカットを作った》
- **OS** 略オペレーティングシステム《コンピュータ・システムの全体を管理するソフトウェア, operating systemの略》
- **oval** 形卵形の, 楕円形の
- **overseas** 名国外
- **ox** 名雄牛

P

- **paid for by** 《be-》~によって支払われる
- **painting** 名絵(をかくこと), 絵画
- **pair** 名(2つから成る)一対, 一組, ペア
- **pajama** 名《通例-s》パジャマ
- **pale** 形(顔色・人が)青ざめた, 青白い
- **Palo Alto** パロアルト《地名》
- **Paramount Pictures** パラマウントピクチャーズ《アメリカの映画会社》

Word List

- **Parker, Sean** (ショーン・)パーカー《インターネット企業家, コンピュータ界では伝説的なハッカー, ナップスターやPlaxoの共同設立者であり, フェイスブックでも活躍した, 1979–》
- **particular** 形 特別の in particular 特に, とりわけ
- **particularly** 副 特に, とりわけ
- **partly** 副 一部分は
- **partner** 名 仲間, 同僚
- **passage** 名 通路
- **past** 形 過去の, この前の
- **patient** 名 病人, 患者
- **pay** 動 支払う, 払う pay no attention 気にしない, 目もくれない
- **payment** 名 支払い
- **PayPal** 名 ペイパル《オンラインでの決済サービスを提供する会社, 1998–》
- **Pennsylvania, University of** 名 ペンシルベニア大学
- **per** 前 ~につき, ~ごとに
- **perhaps** 副 たぶん, おそらく
- **Peter Benchley** ピーター・ベンチリー《映画『ジョーズ』の原作者, 1940–2006》
- **Peter Thiel** ピーター・シール《ペイパルの共同設立者でありCEO, フェイスブック初となる資金投資を行った》
- **Phillips Exeter** フィリップス・エクセター高校《ザッカーバーグが通った有名な進学校》
- **philosophy** 名 哲学, 主義, 信条
- **photo** 名 写真
- **photo-hosting** 名 写真共有, 写真データをウェブ上で預かり運用するサービス
- **photo-sharing** 名 写真をオンラインで共有すること
- **photograph** 名 写真
- **Pirates of the Caribbean** 『パイレーツ・オブ・カリビアン』《ジョニー・デップ主演の海賊映画, 2003, またはそのシリーズ作》
- **pistachio** 名 ピスタチオ
- **plan to** ~するつもりである
- **platform** 名 プラットフォーム《アプリケーション・ソフトを稼働させるための基本ソフト, またはハードウェア環境》
- **platform strategy** プラットフォーム戦略《他社がそれを利用して製品製造やサービス提供を行えるような「プラットフォーム=基盤」をつくり, 社会にとって不可欠の地位, あるいは金の流れの元を押さえようとする戦略》
- **Plaxo** 名 プラクソ《オンラインのアドレス帳機能に特化したソーシャルネットワーキングサービス》
- **play tricks** 策をろうする
- **pleased** 形 喜んだ, 気に入った be pleased with ~が気に入る
- **plenty** 名 たくさん, 豊富
- **poet** 名 詩人, 歌人
- **poker game** 名 (トランプで)ポーカー
- **polite** 形 ていねいな, 礼儀正しい, 洗練された
- **political** 形 政治の, 政治的な
- **politics** 名 政治(学), 政策
- **pool** 名 プール
- **posh** 形 豪華な, 上流階級の
- **positive** 形 前向きな, 肯定的な, 好意的な, プラスの
- **possible** 形 ①可能な ②ありうる, 起こりうる as ~ as possible できるだけ~ make it possible for ~ to … ~が…できるようにする
- **post** 動 (インターネットなどに情報を)載せる, 投稿する
- **potential** 名 可能性, 潜在能力
- **powerful** 形 実力のある, 影響力

The Mark Zuckerberg Story

- **presentation** 名実演, プレゼンテーション
- **presidency** 名大統領職
- **president** 名 ①大統領 ②社長, 学長
- **press** 名出版物[社]
- **pressure** 名プレッシャー, 圧力, 重荷
- **prestigious** 形世評の高い, 名声のある
- **Princeton University** プリンストン大学
- **printing press** 印刷機
- **privacy** 名プライバシー, 個人情報　**privacy setting** プライバシー設定
- **private** 形私的な, 個人の　**private school** 私立学校
- **privileged** 形特権のある
- **probably** 副たぶん, おそらく
- **process** 名手順, 方法, 製法
- **product** 名製品, 産物
- **professional** 形専門の, プロの
- **professor** 名教授
- **profile** 名プロフィール, 人物紹介
- **profit** 名利益, 利潤
- **programmer** 名コンピュータ・プログラマー
- **programming** 名コンピュータ・プログラミング
- **progress** 名 ①進歩, 前進 ②成り行き, 経過
- **project** 名 ①計画, プロジェクト ②研究課題
- **promote** 動宣伝する
- **protest** 動抗議する, 反対する
- **Protestant** 名プロテスタント
- **prototype** 動〜の試作品を作る　名試作品
- **proud** 形自慢の, 誇った　〜を自慢に思う
- **provide** 動供給する
- **psychiatrist** 名精神科医
- **psychology** 名心理学
- **public** 形公開の, 公の　**go public** (企業が)株式を公開する　**public relations** ピーアール, [宣伝]広報活動　**public school** 公立学校
- **publicity** 名宣伝, 広報
- **publish** 動 ①発表[公表]する ②出版[発行]する
- **publishing** 形出版業の
- **punishment** 名罰, 処罰
- **push** 熟 **push communication** プッシュ型通信　**push out** 押し出す, 排除する
- **put on** ①〜を設置する ②〜を…の上に置く

Q

- **question-and-answer** 名質疑応答, 質問と答え
- **quickly** 副すぐに, 敏速に, 急いで
- **quite** 熟 **not quite** まったく〜だというわけではない
- **Quora** 名クオーラ《Q＆Aサービスに特化したソーシャルネットワーキングサービス》

R

- **racist** 名人種差別主義者
- **Randi** 名ランディ《ザッカーバーグの姉, フェイスブックのマーケティングディレクターを務める》
- **rank** 動並べる, ランク付けする
- **rather** 副むしろ, それどころか逆に　**rather than** 〜よりむしろ
- **ready** 熟 **be ready to** すぐに[いつでも]〜できる, 〜する構えで　**get**

112

Word List

- ready 用意[支度]をする
- **reality** 熟 in reality 実は、実際には
- **realize** 動 ①はっきり理解する ②実現する
- **recent** 形 近ごろの
- **receptionist** 名 受付係、フロント係
- **recognize** 動 認識する
- **recommend** 動 推薦する
- **recommendation** 名 推薦(状)
- **record** 名 (音楽などの)レコード
- **reddish-brown** 形 赤みがかった茶色の
- **reduce** 動 減じる
- **refuse** 動 拒絶する、断る
- **register** 動 登録する
- **registration** 名 登録 open registration オープン登録制
- **Reid Hoffman** リード・ホフマン《リンクトイン社の創立者》
- **relate** 動 関連がある、かかわる
- **relation** 名 人間関係、間柄
- **relationship** 名 関係、関連
- **release** 動 発表する、リリースする 名 発表、リリース
- **remain** 動 (〜の)ままである[いる]
- **rent** 動 賃借りする
- **rental** 名 賃貸料
- **rented** 形 賃貸の、賃借りした
- **repaid** 動 repay (払い戻す)の過去、過去分詞
- **reply** 動 答える、返事をする、応答する
- **represent** 動 代表する
- **reputation** 名 評判、世評
- **research** 名 調査、研究
- **respect** 名 尊敬、尊重 動 尊敬[尊重]する
- **restructure** 動 再編成する、再構築する
- **result** 名 結果、成り行き
- **rethought from the ground up** 初めから考え直された
- **return for** 〜に対する見返りとして、〜の交換条件として
- **revenge** 名 復讐 get one's revenge 恨みを晴らす
- **revenue** 名 所得、収入、利益
- **revolution** 名 革命
- **revolutionary** 形 革命の
- **Revolutionary Armed Forces of Colombia** コロンビア革命軍《中南米最大の反政府武装組織、略称FARC》
- **revolutionize** 動 大変革[革命]をもたらす、根本的に変える
- **right now** 今すぐに、たった今
- **rising** 形 上がる、高まる
- **risk** 名 危険
- **rival** 名 競争相手、匹敵する人
- **robotic** 形 機械的な、ロボットのような
- **rock'n'roll** 名 ロックンロール
- **Roman art** ローマ美術
- **roommate** 名 ルームメイト、部屋を共有する相手
- **row** 名 in a row 1列に(並んで)、連続して
- **rowing** 名 ボート、漕艇
- **rubber** 名 ゴム
- **rude** 形 無作法な、失礼な
- **run on** どんどん進む、走り寄る
- **Russia** 名 ロシア《国名》

S

- **salary** 名 給料
- **San Francisco** サンフランシス

コ《米国の都市》
- **sandal** 名《通例-s》サンダル
- **Sandberg, Sheryl**（シェリル・）サンドバーグ《世界銀行や財務省、グーグルなどでキャリアを積んだハーバード卒の女性。2008年にフェイスブックに入社し最高執行責任者を務めた》
- **Saverin, Eduardo**（エドゥアルド・）サベリン《ブラジル人、ハーバード時代にザッカーバーグの共同出資者になる》
- **scholarship** 名 奨学金
- **Sean Parker** ショーン・パーカー《インターネット企業家、コンピュータ界では伝説的なハッカー、ナップスターやPlaxoの共同設立者であり、フェイスブックでも活躍した、1979–》
- **search** 動 捜し求める、調べる
- **seaside** 名 海辺、海岸、浜
- **secondly** 副 第2に、次に
- **secret** 形 秘密の、隠れた
- **secretary** 名 ①秘書 ②《S-》長官、大臣 **treasury secretary** 財務長官
- **security** 名 安全(性)
- **seem** 動（〜に）見える、（〜のように）思われる
- **self-taught** 形 独学の
- **selling** 名 販売、売却
- **semester** 名（前期・後期の）学期
- **seminar** 名 セミナー、研究会
- **senator** 名 上院議員
- **Sequoia Capital** セコイアキャピタル《アメリカの投資会社》
- **serious** 形 まじめな、真剣な、深刻な
- **server** 名 サーバー《コンピュータ・ネットワークにおいて、各コンピュータの要求に答えて機能やデータを供給するコンピュータのこと》
- **service** 名 事業、サービス
- **set up** 配置する、セットする、据え付ける
- **setting** 名 設定 **privacy setting** プライバシー設定
- **Seven** 名『セブン』《映画、1995》
- **sex** 名 性、性別
- **sexist** 名 性別差別をする人、男尊女卑主義者
- **shabby** 形 みすぼらしい、粗末な、貧相な
- **shadow** 動 尾行する、影のようについて回る
- **share** 動 分配する、分担する、共有する 名 株
- **shareholder** 名 株主
- **Sheryl Sandberg** シェリル・サンドバーグ《世界銀行や財務省、グーグルなどでキャリアを積んだハーバード卒の女性。2008年にフェイスブックに入社し最高執行責任者を務めた》
- **shocked** 形 ショックを受けた
- **short-lived** 形 短命の、はかない、長続きしない
- **short-term** 形 短期間の
- **shorts** 名 ショートパンツ
- **showman** 名 演出の巧みな人
- **shut** 動 閉まる、閉める、閉じる、たたむ **shut down** 終了する **shut off** 遮断する、切り離す、除外する
- **shy** 形 内気な、恥ずかしがりの
- **side** 名 側、そば
- **Silicon Valley** シリコンバレー《地名、工業集積地域》
- **silly** 形 おろかな、思慮のない
- **similar** 形 同じような、類似した、相似の
- **simply** 副 ①単に、ただ ②まったく、完全に
- **singer** 名 歌手、シンガー
- **single** 形 それぞれの
- **sixth sense** 第六感

Word List

- **sketch** 動 スケッチする
- **Skype** 名 スカイプ《インターネットを用いた無料通話ができるソフトウェア》
- **slang** 名 俗語, スラング
- **slow down** 速度を落とす
- **slowly** 副 遅く, ゆっくり
- **smartphone** 名 スマートフォン《多機能な携帯電話》
- **smoothly** 副 滑らかに
- **sneakers** 名 スニーカー, 運動靴
- **social** 形 社会の, 社会的な
- **social game** ソーシャル(・ネットワーキング)・ゲーム《SNS上のプレーヤーが交流しながら楽しむオンラインゲーム》
- **social graph** ソーシャルグラフ《ネットユーザー間の関係を示す相関図や情報》
- **social mission** 社会的使命
- **social networking** ソーシャルネットワーキング《特にインターネットを利用して, 友人・知人の輪を広げていくこと》
- **social networking service** ソーシャルネットワーキングサービス《略称SNS, インターネット上で人脈を構築するサービス》
- **social stream** ソーシャルストリーム《ソーシャルの関係性(ソーシャルグラフ)の中を伝わる情報の流れ》
- **society** 名 社会, 世間
- **software** 名 ソフト(ウェア) open source software オープン・ソース・ソフトウエア《ソースプログラムが公開されているソフトウエア》
- **solve** 動 解く, 解決する
- **some days** 《on-》〜する日もある
- **someone** 代 ある人, 誰か
- **something** 代 ある物, 何か
- **sometimes** 副 時々, 時たま
- **sophomore** 名 (4年制大学などの)2年生
- **sort** 名 種類, 品質 a sort of 〜のようなもの, 一種の〜
- **source** 名 源, 情報源 open source software オープン・ソース・ソフトウエア《ソースプログラムが公開されているソフトウエア》
- **sourcing** 名 (情報や部品などの)調達 crowd sourcing クラウドソーシング《不特定多数の人々に無償または低額報酬で(インターネットを介して)仕事を依頼すること》
- **Spanish** 名 スペイン語
- **speaking** 名 話すこと, 談話
- **specialized** 形 専門の, 分化した
- **specially** 副 特に
- **split** 動 裂く, 割る, 分裂させる[する]
- **spokesman** 名 スポークスマン, 代弁者
- **SpongeBob SquarePants Movie** 映画『スポンジボブ・スクエアパンツ』《アメリカ製ギャグアニメ, 『スポンジボブ』の映画版, 2004》
- **square** 名 四角い広場, (市外の)一区画
- **staff** 名 職員, スタッフ
- **Stalkerbook** 名 ストーカーブック《フェイスブックに友人の活動が通知される新システムが搭載され, これを嫌った利用者たちがフェイスブックにつけたあだ名》
- **Stanford University** スタンフォード大学
- **start out** (事業を)始める
- **state** 名 国家, 州
- **stay** 熟 stay in touch 連絡を絶やさない
- **steal** 動 ①盗む ②こっそりと手に入れる, こっそりと〜する 名 盗み, 盗品
- **Steve Jobs** スティーブ・ジョブ

ズ《アップル社の共同設立者の一人, 1955–2011》
- [ ] **stock** 名 株式 stock market 株式市場
- [ ] **stolen** 動 steal（盗む）の過去分詞
- [ ] **strategy** 名 戦略, 作戦, 方針 platform strategy プラットフォーム戦略《他社がそれを利用して製品製造やサービス提供を行えるような「プラットフォーム＝基盤」をつくり, 社会にとって不可欠の地位, あるいは金の流れの元を押さえようとする戦略》
- [ ] **stream** 名 流れ, 風潮
- [ ] **strengthen** 動 強くする, しっかりさせる
- [ ] **stroll** 動 散策する, そぞろ歩く
- [ ] **strongly** 副 強く, 熱心に
- [ ] **structure** 名 構造, 骨組み, 仕組み
- [ ] **student counselor** スチューデント・カウンセラー, 学生相談室相談員
- [ ] **stuff** 名 もの, 材料（小道具）
- [ ] **style** 名 やり方, 様式, スタイル
- [ ] **suburb** 名 近郊, 郊外
- [ ] **succeed** 動 成功する
- [ ] **success** 名 成功, 幸運, 上首尾
- [ ] **successful** 形 成功した, うまくいった
- [ ] **suffer** 動 ①（苦痛・損害などを）受ける, こうむる ②苦しむ, 悩む
- [ ] **suggest** 動 提案する
- [ ] **suite** 名 （ホテルなどの）スイートルーム
- [ ] **summer break** 夏休み
- [ ] **Summers, Lawrence** （ローレンス・）サマーズ《ザッカーバーグ在学中のハーバード大学学長, クリントン政権で財務長官を務めた, 1954–》
- [ ] **SumZero** 名 サムゼロ《投資家たちのためのコミュニケーションネットワーク》
- [ ] **supergroup** 名 スーパーグループ《音楽》
- [ ] **supporter** 名 後援者, 支持者, サポーター
- [ ] **sure** 熟 make sure 確かめる, 確認する not sure if 〜かどうか不明である to be sure 確かに, なるほど
- [ ] **sweatshirt** 名 スエットシャツ, トレーナー
- [ ] **swam** 動 swim（泳ぐ）の過去
- [ ] **switch** 切り替える, 切り替わる
- [ ] **Synapse** 名 シナプス《聴いている音楽の系統を分析し, お勧めの曲を教えてくれる音楽再生ソフト》

T

- [ ] **T-shirt** 名 Tシャツ
- [ ] **tag** 動 札をつける
- [ ] **tagging** 名 タグ付け, 標識付け
- [ ] **tagline** 名 キャッチフレーズ
- [ ] **take** 熟 take a risk リスクを負う, 危険を冒す take into 手につかむ, 中に取り入れる take off（衣服を）脱ぐ, 取り去る, 〜を取り除く, 離陸する, 出発する take one's mind off 〜から心をそらす take over 支配する
- [ ] **talented** 形 才能のある, 有能な
- [ ] **target** 動 的［目標］にする
- [ ] **teaching** 名 授業
- [ ] **tech** 略 技術者の, 科学技術の《technicalの略》
- [ ] **tech giant** 偉大な技術者
- [ ] **technical** 形 技術（上）の
- [ ] **technology** 名 テクノロジー, 科学技術
- [ ] **television** 名 テレビ
- [ ] **term** 名 期間, 期限
- [ ] **terrorist** 名 テロリスト
- [ ] **text** 名 本文, 文章, テキスト

Word List

- **than** 熟 more than ~以上 rather than ~よりむしろ
- **thanks to** ~のおかげで
- **theater** 名 劇場, 映画館
- **Thefacebook** 名 ザフェイスブック《フェイスブック設立当初の名前, 後にThe を取って現在の名前になった》
- **therefore** 副 したがって, それゆえ, その結果
- **Thiel, Peter** (ピーター・) シール《ペイパルの共同設立者でありCEO。フェイスブック初となる資金投資を行った》
- **thinking** 名 考え, 思考
- **three-quarters** 名 四分の三
- **thriller** 名 スリラー物
- **throughout** 副 初めから終わりまで, ずっと
- **Tiananmen Square massacre** 天安門事件, 1989
- **Timeline** 名 タイムライン《フェイスブックの新しい「プロフィール」ページ。投稿, 写真, 行った場所, したことなどがすべて年表形式で表示される》
- **TimeWarner** 名 タイムワーナー《アメリカの総合メディア会社, 1990–》
- **tipping point** 転換期
- **Tom Anderson** トム・アンダーソン《企業家, MySpace社長》
- **tone** 名 口調, 調子
- **tool** 名 道具
- **topic** 名 話題
- **total** 名 全体, 合計
- **touch** 熟 in touch 連絡を取って keep in touch 連絡を取り合う stay in touch 連絡を絶やさない
- **tough** 形 すばらしい
- **town-hall meeting** タウンホールミーティング《出席者との対話を重視した会合》
- **transfer** 動 移動する, 転校する
- **transform** 動 変形 [変化] する, 変える
- **transformation** 名 変化, 変換, 変容
- **translate** 動 翻訳する, 訳す
- **translation** 名 翻訳
- **treasury** 名《the T-》財務省, 大蔵省 treasury secretary 財務長官
- **treat** 動 扱う
- **trendy** 形 流行の, 時代に合った
- **trick** 名 策略 play tricks 策をろうする
- **trouble** 熟 get into trouble 面倒を起こす, 困った事になる, トラブルに巻き込まれる
- **truly** 副 本当に, 実に
- **trust** 動 信用 [信頼] する
- **truth** 名 事実, 真実, 本当
- **Turkey** 名 トルコ《国名》
- **Turkish** 形 トルコ人の
- **turn** 熟 turn into ~に変わる turn on (継続的な供給を) 始める
- **tutor** 名 家庭教師
- **twin** 名 双子の一方, 双生児 identical twins 一卵性双生児
- **Twitter** 名 ツイッター《短いコメントを投稿し合ってコミュニケーションする, ミニブログサービス》
- **Tyler Winkelvoss** タイラー・ウィンクルヴォス《ザッカーバーグに対し, フェイスブックの創設について訴訟を起すウィンクルヴォス双子の一人》
- **type in** (文字を) タイプして入力する
- **typical** 形 典型的な

U

- **U.S. Army** アメリカ陸軍
- **U2** 名 ユーツー《アイルランド出身

のロックバンド》
- □ **ugly** 形 ①ぶかっこうな ②いやな, 不快な
- □ **undergraduate** 名 学部の学生
- □ **underneath** 前 〜の下に, 〜真下に
- □ **unfair** 形 不公平な, 不当な
- □ **unfairly** 副 不当に
- □ **unhappy** 形 不幸な, 不満な
- □ **unique** 形 ユニークな, 独自の
- □ **university** 名 (総合) 大学
- □ **University of Oklahoma** オクラホマ大学
- □ **University of Pennsylvania** ペンシルベニア大学
- □ **unlike** 前 〜と違って
- □ **unpleasant** 形 不愉快な, 気にさわる, いやな, 不快な
- □ **unsuccessful** 形 失敗の, 不成功の
- □ **unusually** 形 異常に
- □ **upgrade** 動 改良する, 向上させる
- □ **uprising** 名 反乱, 暴動, 謀反
- □ **upset** 形 憤慨して 動 気を悪くさせる, (心・神経など)をかき乱す
- □ **URL** 略 ウェブ上の情報の所在を示すコード, 住所のようなもの《Uniform Resource Locatorの略》
- □ **used** 動《 – to》よく〜したものだ, 以前は〜であった
- □ **user** 名 使用者, 利用者, 消費者 **user experience** ユーザー体験
- □ **usual** 形 通常の, いつもの, 平常の, 普通の
- □ **utility** 名《 -ties》公共サービス《ガス, 電気, 水道など》

V

- □ **valuable** 形 貴重な, 価値のある, 役に立つ
- □ **value** 名 価値, 値打ち, 価格 **core value** 基本理念 動 評価する, 値をつける
- □ **VC** 略 投資会社《venture capital firmの略》
- □ **venture** 動 思い切って〜する, 危険にさらす 名 冒険(的事業), 危険
- □ **venture capital firm [company]** 投資会社
- □ **version** 名 バージョン, 版
- □ **Viacom** 名 バイアコム《アメリカのメディアグループ, MTVやパラマウントピクチャーズなどを傘下に持つ》
- □ **viewpoint** 名 観点, 見解
- □ **villain** 名 悪党, 悪者
- □ **Virgil** 名 バージル(ヴェルギリウス)《古代ローマの詩人》
- □ **visionary** 名 夢想家, 夢を追う人
- □ **visitor** 名 訪問客
- □ **visualization** 名 視覚化, 目に見えるようにすること
- □ **vKontakte** 名 フコンタクテ《ロシアで強い人気を誇るソーシャルネットワーキングサービス》
- □ **vote** 動 投票する, 投票して決める
- □ **vs.** 略 (競技や訴訟などで) 対, 〜に対する《versusの略》

W

- □ **Wall** 名 ウォール《フェイスブックのメイン画面で, フェイスブック上の発言や活動を一覧できる》
- □ **Wall Street** ウォール街《米国金融市場, 米国金融業界》
- □ **warn** 動 警告する, 用心させる
- □ **Washington Post** ワシントンポスト《1877年に創刊されたアメリカの新聞, またはそれを発行している会社》

Word List

- **WASP（White Anglo-Saxon Protestant）** ワスプ《ホワイト・アングロサクソン・プロテスタントの略．アメリカ合衆国の白人エリート層の保守派．または白人を指す》
- **way** 熟 in a way ある意味では way to ～する方法
- **wealthy** 形 裕福な，金持ちの
- **wearing** 形 ～を着た姿で
- **website** 名 ウェブサイト，インターネット上の情報が公開されている場所
- **week** 熟 once a week 週に一回
- **well** 熟 as well as ～と同様に
- **well-timed** 形 好機を捉えた，ちょうど良いタイミングの
- **West Wing, The** 『ザ・ホワイトハウス』《ホワイトハウスを舞台に，大統領とその側近たちを描いた政治ドラマ，1999–2006》
- **whatever** 代《関係代名詞》～するものは何でも 形 どんな～でも
- **whenever** 接 ～するたびに
- **wherever** 接 どこでも，どこへ［で］～するとも
- **whether** 接 ～かどうか
- **whiteboard** 名 ホワイトボード《マジックで書いたり消したりできる白い板》
- **whole** 形 全体の，すべての，完全な 名《the-》全体，全部
- **whomever** 代（する）誰にでも
- **willing** 形 喜んで～する，いとわず～する
- **Winkelvoss twins** ウィンクルヴォス双子兄弟《ザッカーバーグに対し，フェイスブックの創設について訴訟を起す兄弟》
- **Wirehog** 名 ワイヤーホグ《情報をインターネット上で共有するためのソフトウェアプログラム》
- **wish** 熟 I wish that nobody had ～．だれも～しないでくれたらよかったのに．《仮定法》
- **Work Networks** ワーク・ネットワークス《どこで働いているかを共有するネットワーク機能》
- **workaholic** 名 仕事の虫，ワーカホリック
- **worldwide** 形 世界的な，世界規模の 副 世界中で
- **worried** 形 心配そうな，不安げな
- **worse** 副 いっそう悪く
- **worst** 副 最も悪く，いちばんひどく
- **worth** 形 （～の）価値がある
- **writer** 名 書き手，作家

Y

- **Y2M** 名 フェイスブックでの広告料を稼ぐことを目的に立ち上げた会社
- **Yahoo!** 名 ヤフー《検索エンジンやポータルサイトなどインターネット関連事業を行う企業，1995–》
- **Yale University** イェール大学
- **youth** 名 若者

Z

- **Zappos** 名 ザッポス《靴を中心としたアパレル関連の通販サイト》
- **Zuck** 名 ザック《ザッカーバーグの愛称》
- **Zuckerberg, Mark Elliot**（マーク・エリオット・）ザッカーバーグ《フェイスブック創立者，1984–》
- **Zucknet** 名 ザックネット《少年ザッカーバーグが父親の医院のために作った来客を通知するプログラム》
- **Zynga** 名 ジンガ《主にフェイスブック上で動くゲームを開発・運営している会社，2007–》

E-CAT

English **C**onversational **A**bility **T**est
国際英語会話能力検定

● E-CATとは…
英語が話せるようになるためのテストです。インターネットベースで、30分であなたの発話力をチェックします。

www.ecatexam.com

iTEP

● iTEP®とは…
世界各国の企業、政府機関、アメリカの大学300校以上が、英語能力判定テストとして採用。オンラインによる90分のテストで文法、リーディング、リスニング、ライティング、スピーキングの5技能をスコア化。iTEP®は、留学、就職、海外赴任などに必要な、世界に通用する英語力を総合的に評価する画期的なテストです。

www.itepexamjapan.com

ラダーシリーズ
The Mark Zuckerberg Story
Facebookを創った男：ザッカーバーグ・ストーリー

2012年6月3日　第1刷発行
2023年4月6日　第9刷発行

著　者　トム・クリスティアン

発行者　浦　晋亮

発行所　IBCパブリッシング株式会社
　　　　〒162-0804 東京都新宿区中里町29番3号
　　　　菱秀神楽坂ビル
　　　　Tel. 03-3513-4511　Fax. 03-3513-4512
　　　　www.ibcpub.co.jp

© IBC Publishing, Inc. 2012

印刷　株式会社シナノパブリッシングプレス
装丁　伊藤 理恵
組版データ　Sabon Roman + Bernard MT Condensed Regular

落丁本・乱丁本は、小社宛にお送りください。送料小社負担にてお取り替えいたします。本書の無断複写 (コピー) は著作権法上での例外を除き禁じられています。

Printed in Japan
ISBN978-4-7946-0145-2